D1459827

A BOOK OF PLAYS

BY WITTER BYNNER

NEW YORK
ALFRED · A · KNOPF
MCMXXII

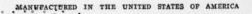

CONTENTS

NOTE

Tiger and *The Little King* and the Choruses from *Iphigenia* appeared originally in The Forum—and *Cycle* in The Stratford Magazine.

The translation of *Iphigenia* was made for Isadora Duncan.

*To Homer and Carlota Saint-
Gaudens and their Little Boy*

Time: The morning of October 16, 1793.

Scene: In the Temple at Paris: a room in which is imprisoned Louis XVII, the Boy-King of France, under the tutelage of Antoine Simon and his wife, Jeanne Marie.

Behind a large iron-barred door at the back is an anteroom from which one staircase descends to the courtyard and another ascends to a platform on the roof of the Temple. A closed door leads at the left into a bedroom. Near it stands an elaborate bird-cage in which a wooden canary moves when wound up and whistles " The March of the King." In the cage are also some live canaries, one of which has a red ribbon round its neck. A small barred window at the right overlooks the courtyard. Under it are a box of mortar and some squared stones, one or two of which have al-

7

*ready been set into the window. Nearby is a
table, a cupboard of dishes and on the floor
a basket of soiled linen.*

*At rise of the curtain, Jeanne Marie, with
a dish in her hand, stands by a larger table
where three people have just finished a light
meal. She is a squat woman of fifty with
thick features and a blotched face. While she
clears the table, she talks with Barelle, appar-
ently a middle-aged stonemason, who is mix-
ing mortar with his trowel near the window.*

JEANNE

[*As she carries soiled dishes into the anteroom*]
What?—Block the door and shut out all the
  light?

BARELLE

The window first and afterward both doors.
A grating left there for his meals, but not
An aperture for light or hope or mercy.

JEANNE

Ah, but the fools have chosen you to do
The job! Luck's with us, Citizen Barelle.

BARELLE

You mean God's with us. God himself,
not they,

Selected me,—to be His instrument.

JEANNE

There's damnable divinity in gold.

You be the God. I'll be the instrument.

BARELLE

[*Removing from the window a cross-shaped
iron bar*]

O Father, prove Thy greatness to these
people

That have turned coward toward a little
boy,

Son of the King they killed! O Lord, reach
down

Thy hand to us! For Jesus' sake, Thy Son,

Give me Thy strength to save the Son of
France!

JEANNE

[*Seizing the iron bar*]

Here's holy water for your crucifix.

[*She spits on it and throws it on the floor*]

BARELLE

God pity you.——By noon I shall be back
And I shall bring the boy. Does the King
  know?

JEANNE

Leave that to me. You fetch the other King.
And, please, the puppy-dog has learned his
  change
Of name. Not King, not Louis any more!
Just call him Capet and he'll wag his tail
With quite remarkable intelligence.

BARELLE

How are you going to manage with Michel?

JEANNE

Michel relieves the other guard at noon.
As soon as he's alone he'll signal us.

BARELLE

Your husband——

JEANNE

          Leave my husband to your God!
Leave everything to God—except His Image;

Soon as the coin comes round—leave that
   to me;
And while we're talking—what about the
   coin?

BARELLE
One payment now.   The rest as we agreed.

JEANNE
God in three parts!   And one part now!
   Come pay it!

BARELLE
[*Taking from inside his blouse a bag of
gold, which he hands to her*]
And you at noon pay me my King!
[*Exit Barelle*]

JEANNE
[*To the bag of gold*]
     Sweet God!
[*She kisses it, then hides it in her sewing-
basket on the small table. Humming a snatch
of the Marseillaise, she throws open the bedroom door and calls through it with her
arms akimbo*]

Capet, your eyes are red.   Go scrub your
   face.
Make it all red like a washerlady's son.

THE KING
   [*A boy of nine, his voice heard outside*]
   I am a Queen's son!

JEANNE
      Times have changed, my dear,
   And Marie Antoinette has handkerchiefs
   To wash, she cries so much.   Her nose now
      looks
   Like anyone's and gets as red as mine.

THE KING
   It is not red.

JEANNE
      Go make yours red, Capet!
   For you're to be a washerlady's son
   This very day.—Sh-h!   Don't you tell An-
      toine!
   [*She hears him on his way upstairs singing
   a revolutionary chant.   She quickly closes the*

bedroom door and turns toward the ante-
room where Antoine Simon enters. He is
a big shoemaker of fifty-five, with straight
black hair hanging long and a swarthy brut-
ish face. He carries aloft two bottles of
brandy]

ANTOINE
I've brought two friends with me.

JEANNE
[*Seizing a corkscrew*]
          Off with their heads!

ANTOINE
Let go my friends! I bring 'em here like
   this
And you—you murder 'em! You used to be
A stylish drinker, Jeanne Marie. But now
You're an old soak.

JEANNE
          Only a soak would talk
Like that. I taste my glass the same as ever.
It's you who booze like a lout and waste a
   lot
On Capet, just to make the poor brat drunk.

ANTOINE

You're keen to see him caper round, yourself.
But you don't pay your share. You get two-
   thirds
As much as me for staying in this hole
And you never spend a sou.
[*He sits and changes his boots for slippers*]

JEANNE

[*Carrying dishes from table to cupboard*]
         The nation takes
Good care of you, husband,—also of me:
Six thousand livres your share, four thou-
   sand mine.

ANTOINE

A patriotic cobbler and his wife
Cooped up like marquises!

JEANNE

         You make me sick,
Talking like that about ten thousand livres.
You don't know what you want, you lucky
   fool.

ANTOINE

> Know what I want?   I want to be let off
> From tutoring Capet.   But let me off
> They won't.   They've got me here.   And
>   here I stick
> And rot.   It's bad for the brain, that's
>   what it is.
> Capet's much luckier than we are, Jeanne,
> For he has us, he has, for company,
> But we have only him.

> [*The King, a handsome, gentle boy, appears
> at the bedroom door. Antoine hurls his boot
> at the King*]

>   Get out of here!

> [*The King looks calmly at them both, then
> returns into the bedroom. Jeanne Marie
> closes the door after him*]

JEANNE

> [*In a superstitious whisper*]
> He looked at me as my boy Raymond did.
> He looked at me as my dead Raymond
>   did.

ANTOINE

Forget your Raymond! Capet isn't Raymond.

JEANNE

You're sore because he waked you up last night.

ANTOINE

With his damn prayers! I fixed him good. He'll not
Be trying Trappist tricks on me again.

JEANNE
[*Angrily*]
Yes, fixed him good and maybe fixed yourself.
Doused him with water, let him lie between
The icy sheets and shiver all night long!
What if he's caught his death?

ANTOINE

What did they say
When I asked 'em, the Committee, about Capet,

Whether they wanted me to poison him?
They said, 'Well, don't you let him grow too
   much!'
Wife dear, what did they mean?

JEANNE
       They meant, 'Don't add
A cubit to his stature,—cut him short,
But not too short!' They know their busi-
   ness best.
Why do you suppose they send a mason
   here?

ANTOINE
Barelle, you mean?

JEANNE
      To seal that window up.

ANTOINE
Make bats of us?

JEANNE
     No, not of us. Of him!
They're going to block the door and lock
   him in.

ANTOINE
  And lock us out?

JEANNE
      We'll feed him through a hole
  Cut here and talk to him an hour a day.

ANTOINE
  On what?

JEANNE
      On Liberty.

ANTOINE
      Woman, he'll live
  For years.

JEANNE
      O no, my dove, he's delicate.

ANTOINE
  But I've a mind to do for him today
  And end this job.

JEANNE
      You're good at jokes on death.

Our Lady Guillotine might yet arrange
A joke on you. And, citizen, I fear
You wouldn't laugh so well without your
mouth.

ANTOINE
But I don't see who'd care about a Capet.

JEANNE
Because they had no use for Louis Capet?
Because they say about the Austrian,
"Why does she ask for cake, when there is
dust
To eat"? But people have soft hearts.
They might
Forgive the boy his dirty breed, Antoine.
A child's a child, no matter from what stock.
Besides France has her enemies abroad
Who call the whelp a king. France has her
game
To play. And this one Louis—see?—this
poor
Thin undecipherable piece may be
A lucky coin. I grasp it all so clearly.
And I tell you, Antoine, clever as you are,

When the Council General sent the Simons
here,
They put their trust as a matter of fact—
in me.

ANTOINE
You put your trust in your four thousand
livres
All right, but drink your brandy on my pay,
On the six thousand which they give to me
For being less important than my wife.

JEANNE
A child's head looks ridiculous on a pike.

ANTOINE
No, it looks neat.

JEANNE
Hey, Antoine, listen! Drums.

ANTOINE
Some one they've got to guillotine, I guess.

JEANNE
The roof, the platform! Call if you can see!

ANTOINE
I'll bet you first it's Marie Antoinette.

JEANNE
An end of her? Not on your life, my dear!
If it were women trying her, then yes.
But this Tribunal? Men, Antoine? Not
much!

ANTOINE
Justice decides and Justice is a female!

JEANNE
They'll feast for days upon those dainty eyes
Before the garbage goes. If she's a beauty—
I hope I'm not.

ANTOINE
You're not.

JEANNE
Trust her with men?
She's got you, all of you, just where you're
weak—
She'd charm the hind leg off the Lamb o'
God!

ANTOINE

Bet me the brandy on it?—the cost of the
brandy?

JEANNE

Double the cost!   It's not the Widow Capet.

ANTOINE

[*At the window*]
I'll ask Michel.   He'll know.   He's just
come on.

JEANNE

O husband, how I wish the Guillotine
Was near, where we could watch, to cheer
us up!
In seven weeks I haven't seen one head.
[*Antoine goes upstairs through the anteroom.   Jeanne Marie rapidly takes a piece
of soiled linen and wrapping her bag of
money tightly so that it shall not jingle, lays
the bundle aside on the little table.   Then
she enters the anteroom and calls to her husband*]
Who wins, Antoine?

ANTOINE
> [*Outside*]
>   I do! I win!

JEANNE
>   The Queen?

ANTOINE
> [*Entering*]
> I heard 'em shouting, " Death to Madam
>   Veto! "
> At noon they'll split her like an angle worm!
> Hustle him out. I've news for him.

JEANNE
>   No, no,
> Not yet—he's sick! And when his father
>   croaked
> He wouldn't eat, was like to die himself.
> Go easy, Antoine, for he's off his feed.
> You don't know what might happen. This'll
>   keep.
> You'll have the fun. I'll not sneak in ahead.

ANTOINE
> The brandy, open it. No, pay me first!

[*He opens a bottle. She reluctantly pays him, taking the money from her stocking*]
I tell you what we'll do. We'll make him
    drink.
And then we'll make him dance, dance to the
    bells,
The bells that ring when they lift up her
    head!
That's one on you, old girl! Now fetch
    the brat,
We'll celebrate.

JEANNE
   [*Opening the door*]
       Capet!   Aristocrat!

ANTOINE
   What are you doing?   Eating up those pears
   You took from lunch so's not to eat with us?
   Come out here!   Join your betters!

JEANNE
       Careful now!
   [*The King enters from the bedroom. He has in his hands two pears, which he lays on a chair. Jeanne Marie intercepts Antoine*]

Come here, Capet, I want to tell you something:
A caller's coming—Citizen Barelle.

THE KING
You told me that.

ANTOINE
You like him, don't you?

THE KING
No.

ANTOINE
You do, you little liar.

THE KING
No, I don't.

ANTOINE
Why do you lie to me?

THE KING
I do not like him.

JEANNE
> Have you forgotten that he brought you
> these?
> You like your birds, you ought to like him
> too.

THE KING
> [*After a pause*]
> But if I did, they would not let him come.

ANTOINE
> Your tutor, Simon, never goes away.
> They let him come.

JEANNE
> You're fond of him, ain't you?

ANTOINE
> Come, answer us! You love me, don't you?

THE KING
> Yes.

ANTOINE
> You little liar!

THE KING
> Why do you ask me then?

JEANNE
D'you like me, Capet?

THE KING
Where's my Mama-Queen?
She isn't walking up there any more.
I listen and I listen. Is she sick?
Where have they taken her?

ANTOINE
Don't use that word!

JEANNE
Don't you say Queen! Your tutor doesn't
like it.

THE KING
Where is she gone?

JEANNE
She's sick.

THE KING
I thought she was.
O can't I go to her? Please can't I go
To her?

JEANNE

Not much!

THE KING

Then can't I send her these?
O can't I? Can't I send her my canaries?

JEANNE

You haven't heard that Citizen Barelle
Will bring Robert, the washerwoman's boy,
To stay a little while and play with you?

THE KING

O Master, let me send her my canaries?

ANTOINE

Sit down. We're going to celebrate. Three
glasses!

[*Jeanne Marie brings the glasses*]

THE KING

I do not care for one.

ANTOINE

Sit down, I say!
Here's to the Guillotine! Pick up your
glass.

[*The King draws back*]
Do you want it down your neck? The Guil-
  lotine!
And my good-luck! Come on now.
[*Antoine and Jeanne Marie drink, then he
makes the King drink*]

THE KING
      What good-luck?

JEANNE
  [*With a moment of pity*]
  It's better luck than you would understand.

ANTOINE
  I won a bet, young man. I won that wine.

JEANNE
  And it's a happy day in the Republic!

THE KING
  If it's a really happy day, I'm glad.

ANTOINE
  Then drink to France!—Our Lady Guillo-
    tine
  Drinks blood today to France!

THE KING
  Who is it now?

JEANNE
  [*Preventing Antoine from telling*]
  People you know who used to be at Court.

ANTOINE
  There's no more Court.

THE KING
        O dear, why do they kill
  Good people,—only good, kind people?
    Why?

ANTOINE
  Dunno. They have a funny way with them.
  They'll take me next.

THE KING
        They'll never take you, Master.

ANTOINE
  Ain't you the little joker! Catch your ball!
  Why don't you hold your hands out, blun-
    derhead?
  Can't even learn to catch a ball! We'll see

If you can sing. You know! Your favorite!
[*He sings, Jeanne Marie joining him*]
> Madam Veto thought she could
> Make all Paris run with blood;
> But it didn't come off,
> Thanks to a cough—
> (Dance, dance the Carmagnole!)
> Thanks to a cough—
> Of the cannon!
Put spirit in it, Capet.   Now! Pipe up!

THE KING
" Madam Veto thought she—— " O no, no!
I cannot sing that song.

ANTOINE
> Why not?

THE KING
> Because
You mean my Mother.   And it isn't true.
She hasn't done them any harm.   She loves
Her people, Mother does.

ANTOINE
> She loves her wolves,

Her Austrians!   Her people aren't the
French.

THE KING
Her people are the French.   She told me so.

ANTOINE
You going to sing?

THE KING
How can I sing it, Master?
I cannot sing bad songs about my Mother.

ANTOINE
You sang it yesterday.

THE KING
Master, I didn't.

ANTOINE
Didn't he, Jeanne Marie?

JEANNE
Of course he did.

THE KING
I didn't.

ANTOINE

       Little fool, you don't know what
You do. Get drunk. Here, get a jag again
And sing! You're jolly when you're drunk.
To France!

THE KING

O no, no, no!—not if I sang that song!
What if my Mother heard me sing that
    song?

ANTOINE

She's heard you sing it! Sure she has! It's
    done
Her good, shown her how well I keep my
    word:
' He shall receive a royal education;
We shall instruct him to forget the past
And only to remember he's a child
Of the one and indivisible Republic.'
You sing your song. You won't? Then
    take this drink.
The young wolf shuts his teeth. See, Jeanne
    Marie,

What savage little teeth! He must be
    tamed.
Where's there a knife to pry them open
    with?
We'll cure his pride. Now will you sing
    that song?
Down on your knees! Learn this——

JEANNE
      Let him alone.

ANTOINE
Obedience comes first in Simon's course.
[*He forces the King to the floor*]
Open your mouth. Drink this. Well then,
    try this,
Try this!

JEANNE
      Antoine! Give me that knife!
[*She takes it from him*]

ANTOINE
      Get up.
[*He roughly lifts the motionless King*]
Open your mouth and say you ask my pardon

And we'll postpone the music-lesson. What?
Won't talk?
[*Jeanne Marie turns toward the anteroom,
where Barelle enters, followed by Robert,
who, looking like the King in height, color
and feature, brings a basket of clean clothes
and a bouquet of roses tied with the tricolor.
They see Antoine about to strike the King
with the cross-shaped iron bar*]

BARELLE
You dog!   Is that good tutelage?

JEANNE
For insolence it is!

ANTOINE
The little snob,
I couldn't make him drink the health of
France!

THE KING
(*Grasping the glass*)
You lie!—To France!
[*As he holds the brandy high and then
drinks, the bells ring out*]

JEANNE
        The bells!

ANTOINE
        She's dead! She's dead!
    The holiday! The Carmagnole! She's
    dead!

THE KING
    What do you say? I'm dizzy. France is
    dead?

JEANNE
    France that was crucified—has come to life!

ANTOINE
    The resurrection! Dance, my darling,
    dance!
    [*They start singing the Marseillaise and
    take his hands*]

THE KING
    No!—not to that tune! Wait and I will
    dance.
    [*He breaks away and turns on the catch
    which sets the toy canary whistling*]

I'll dance to my tune, mine!—The March
of the King!
[*Jeanne Marie turns off the catch*]

BARELLE
[*Interposing between Antoine's anger and
the King*]
Go slowly, Citizen, to cure a King.
The lilies flourished for a thousand years.
Uprooting them takes time.

JEANNE
          Well,—time takes root.

BARELLE
How are your birds, Capet?

ANTOINE
          They sing, but he?—
He has the pip!

BARELLE
[*Crossing to work at the window*]
          I left an officer
Behind me on the stairs whose legs were
weak

With too much holiday. He's bound, he
  says,
' To mourn the dead with Citizen Simon.'

JEANNE
  [*Handing Antoine the bottle and glasses*]
  Here! Comfort him! The platform's pleas-
    anter.
  [*While Barelle fits a stone into the window,
  Jeanne Marie sees Antoine out and closes
  the heavy door after him*]

THE KING
  [*Politely to Jeanne Marie*]
  He doesn't understand about the window.
  You said that he was going to mend the
    window.

JEANNE
  That's what he's doing. There were holes
    in it.

BARELLE
  Let's see which one is taller of you boys.
  [*They measure back to back*]

ROBERT

We're just the same.

THE KING

Why, yes, we're just the same.
[*Receiving from Robert the bunch of roses*]
Thank you, Robert.

ROBERT

I thought you'd like them. Look!
Look underneath the roses,—look at this!

THE KING

My flower, my flower!

BARELLE

A lily for the King.
[*The King kisses the lily and hides it again
under the roses*]

THE KING

Sir, you've been kind to me both times you've
come.
Last time you brought me my canary-birds.
I have not anything to give to you
But these two pears which I have saved from
lunch.

And, just because I am so poor, I beg
That you will please me, sir, by taking one.
And will you take the other one, Robert!

BARELLE
I thank your Majesty.

JEANNE
　　　　Get up! Don't call
Him that. It isn't done. You're right, they are
As like as peas. Listen to me, Capet.
Take off your things. Put on Robert's.

THE KING
　　　　What for?

JEANNE
[*On guard near the big door*]
You're going to be Robert. Obey Barelle,
Do everything he says. For, if you don't,
They'll kick you, whip you and cut off your head.

BARELLE
You'll come with me?

THE KING

        I'll go with you and do
Just what you tell me to.   But afterwards
They'll punish me.

BARELLE

        You do not understand.
We are your friends.   We come to free you,
   Sire.

THE KING
  My Mother too?—my Mother?

BARELLE

        Where you go,
The Queen shall follow you.   Be sure of
  that.

THE KING
  Then take me to her!   That will make me
  sure.

BARELLE
  Robert, your coat!
  [*Robert takes off his coat and waits by the
  bedroom door*]

THE KING
    I think you are my friend.

JEANNE
    [*Showing and patting her bundle*]
    He's counted out the proof of it in cash.
    He's paid me money. Think of it, for you!—
    A little piece of rotten meat like you!

BARELLE
    [*To Jeanne Marie*]
    You are the rotten meat I purchased!

JEANNE
        Pooh!
    Don't wave your crest at me, old cockatoo!

THE KING
    You mean that you have had to pay for me?

ROBERT
    Come quick, for we must change our clothes,
        you know.

THE KING
    [*To Robert, in the doorway*]
    Mother will look at me that funny way

And not know which to do, to laugh or cry,
And not do either—but just look at me.
Doesn't your mother look at you like that?

ROBERT
Come, little King, and change our clothes.

THE KING
          Mine does.
[*He follows Robert into the bedroom*]

BARELLE
You'll watch the door?

JEANNE
[*Opening the big door a crack*]
          The platform-stairway creaks.
I always hear him coming.

BARELLE
[*Looking through the window*]
          What?—Two guards?

JEANNE
We'll have to wait till Michel's there alone,
Before you start.
[*She sits and sews listening by the big door*]

BARELLE

[*Setting another stone in place, watching*]
> I wish that you had told Antoine.

JEANNE

> I'm no such fool. I know Antoine.
> He would have shilly-shallied half-a-year.
> Antoine's a coward. If I do the thing,
> Saving him all the pains and half the cash,
> He'll thank me when it's done. I know
>   Antoine.

BARELLE

> He may come down.

JEANNE

> Then let me manage him,
> Bottle him up again and think for him
> And act for him,—and put a sum away
> With which to make him love me by-and-by.

BARELLE

> How little you have learned from our mis-
>   take!
> You care for him by caring for his money

As we took care of you by keeping yours.—
There would have been no need of blood
    and tears,
If only my poor friends had counted well
And learned the deadly peril of too much
And dared to be contented with enough.

JEANNE

Enough is not enough and never will be.
I tell you, Citizen, there's no such thing
As coin enough. Look at the two of us!—
You've had too much and you philosophize.
I've had too little and I kick up hell.
But those who have enough—lie in their
    graves.
Too much, too little—life! Enough—the
    end.
[*The boys enter, each in the other's clothes.
The King has Robert's liberty cap in his
hand*]

THE KING

I have on everything. But not the cap!

JEANNE

Put that on too. No matter where you go,

You'll never wear a crown in France again.
Put that on too, my darling Citizen.
[*The King still holds it in his hand*]

BARELLE
Run back again, if anyone should come,
And change the jackets—that would do.

JEANNE
        And then
Come out again like you'd been playing ball.
Here, Capet, take it, have it in your pocket.
When Michel's by himself, Barelle, don't
    wait
To talk. Just go. See, Capet, there's your
    load.
I've lightened it,—so's not to strain your
    wings.
[*She sits and sews again by the big door.
The King tries the weight of the basket,
then lays it down and stands watching Rob-
ert. Presently he takes Robert by the hand
and leads him to the cage of canaries*]

THE KING
[*Softly*]
I like the one you gave me best of all.

My toy canary sings 'The March of the
   King'
And the one you gave me tries to copy him.

[*They sit on the floor by the cage*]

I've tied a little ribbon on his neck
To tell him by.—I think he knows me,
   Robert.
He lets me take him out of the cage and
   talk
To him. And he turns his head and looks.
   And once
He sang to me sitting right on my finger.
O how I wish my Mama-Queen could see
   him!
They wouldn't let me send him up to her.
She's sick and ought to have all sorts of
   things
To comfort her.—Perhaps they'll let me
   send
My flowers to her. Wouldn't you like to
   have me?
To comfort her, Robert, instead of me,
Because she's sick, you know?

ROBERT

> Yes, little King.

THE KING

> I do not like to have you call me King.
> They might not let you play with me
> again. . . .
> And then besides it means my Father's dead.

ROBERT

> The King is dead,—long live the Little
> King!

THE KING

> The night he left he took me on his knee
> And held my hand and made me swear,
> Robert,
> That I'd forgive his people everything
> And not be harsh with them when I grow up.
> And don't you think that that was like Our
> Savior?
> Next day my Mother helped me pray for
> him;
> But when I tried to think of the good God,
> I couldn't think of anyone but Papa.
> Why did they kill him, Robert?

ROBERT

      Mother says
Because their hearts are bronze.

THE KING

      I told my Father,
The day I lost Moufflet, my dog, the day
We came to the Temple and the men stuck
    out
Their tongues and knocked the statue down
    and called
My Mother names, I told my Father then
How bad they were. But he said, ' No, they
    weren't.'
He said that they would understand him
    some day
And find that we were just like them and ask
Our pardon for the way they treated us.
You ought to have seen how Mama looked
    at him!
And then she kissed him. Then she kissed
    me, too
And cried, Robert, because I think she knew
Better than Papa what was happening.
There's nobody so wonderful as Mama.

Why do they call her names and sing bad
    songs
About her, when she's good?   My Mother's
    good.
She doesn't hate the people.

JEANNE
        Shut your mouth,
Capet, and pay attention!   Watch Barelle!

BARELLE
He will not go, the man will never go!—
Hast Thou forgotten us?

JEANNE
        Don't drag in God.
Just wait and watch and, when the time
    comes, act.
You'll learn some day there isn't any God.
[*They all wait a moment or two, silent*]

THE KING
[*Whispering, close to Robert*]
When I was little, Mama had her hair
Away up high with a hundred waves in it.
And on the waves were tiny ships, Robert!

O it was wonderful! She waked me up
To let me see it.—And I had a sword.

JEANNE

[*Jumping to her feet*]
He's coming! Quick, the both of you, get in
   there!
[*The boys run into the bedroom. Jeanne
Marie shuts them in, then sits again and
sews. Barelle works at the window*]

ANTOINE

[*Entering*]
We want another bottle of that brandy.

JEANNE

Here, take it. Drink it up. To hell with
   Queens!

ANTOINE

What's the son of the she-wolf doing, hey?
[*To Barelle*]
I'm not supposed to take my eye off him,
You know. Even asleep, one eye must be
Propped up and watching him. A pretty job!
Where is he?

JEANNE

Here's your bottle.

ANTOINE

[*Brushing her aside and opening the door of the bedroom*]
Come on out
Of there!
[*Stopping short, then turning savagely*]
What's this, Barelle?

BARELLE

What, Citizen?

ANTOINE

They're changing coats!—Barelle, what game is this?

JEANNE

If brandy makes a muddle in your brain——

ANTOINE

Come out here, you two!
[*The King enters, his coat in his hand*]
Both of you!
[*Robert follows, cap on but carrying his coat*]

By God!——
What is this game you're playing?

ROBERT
          Citizen——

THE KING
We're playing ball.

ANTOINE
          Show me the ball.

THE KING
[*Finding it in the pocket of his coat*]
          It's here.

ANTOINE
[*Knocking it out of the King's hand*]
Ball in a room that hasn't any light!
What were you changing clothes for?—tell
     me that!

THE KING
We changed our jackets. He didn't want
     to, Master.
I made him play a game of masquerade.

ANTOINE
    The hell you did!
    [*He seizes the King by the throat*]

BARELLE
            Let him alone!   Hands off!

ANTOINE
    Not hands off!   Heads off! And yours first,
        Barelle!

JEANNE
    Yours second, Antoine!

ANTOINE
            Hold your dirty lip!
    You're in on it!

JEANNE
            You lose your head like this
    To-day, you'll lose it good to-morrow. Fool!
    What do you mean to do?

ANTOINE
            Accuse Barelle.

JEANNE
    And me?

ANTOINE

        And you—and get ten thousand
  livres
For taking care of Capet by myself!

JEANNE

  Try it and see! You send me to the scaffold,
  I'll just turn round and take you with me,
    dear.
  You broke the rules, left Capet with Ba-
    relle
  And kept the officer outside. Why that?—
  The reason was a hundred thousand livres!

ANTOINE

  What's this? What hundred thousand?

JEANNE

  [*Lifting her bundle from the table and
  letting it drop back clinking*]
        Use your ears.

BARELLE

  I've sixty thousand here in Paris,—yours!
  This ring! The Prince of Condé's. Take
    him this,

He'll pay the rest.   Now, sir! your life is
   more
To you than mine to me.   I've got you there.
But you can save yours, mine,—and earn,
   besides,
Another hundred thousand livres.

JEANNE
      That is—
Besides my hundred thousand?

BARELLE
      Yes.

JEANNE
      Good God!

BARELLE
Nobody ever comes who knows the King.

JEANNE
And I'll fall sick and we can get away.

BARELLE
With all the cash you need for all your lives.

JEANNE

> Antoine, that means as much as ten whole
>   years
> Of prison and the brat.   Go on upstairs!

ANTOINE

> You should have let me in on this before.

JEANNE

> Shut up with your ' before '!   It's ' now.'
>   Go on!
> That's all you've got to do.   Go on up-
>   stairs!

ANTOINE

> Well, I don't know.   I guess I'd better do it.

JEANNE

> Here!   You're forgetting what you came to
>   fetch.
> [*She hands him the second bottle of brandy*]

ANTOINE

> [*Brandishing it at Barelle*]
> I'd like to smash your head, you Royalist!

BARELLE
God knows, my hand would like——

JEANNE
Quit quarrelling.
I'll see if Michel's there alone.—He is!
Go! Go!

BARELLE
Give me your jacket! Quick, Robert!
Come! and be careful, O be careful, Sire!

THE KING
[*As they put him into Robert's coat*]
My little birds, good-bye. Good-bye, Robert.
My Mother-Queen will bless you when I tell
    her.—
O shall I see green trees again and sky
Spread out?—O think of it—the sky spread
    out!

ROBERT
And lots of birds!

BARELLE
Good-bye, Robert.

ROBERT

Good-bye.

BARELLE

You are a brave and darling boy, Robert.

ROBERT

Good-bye, good-bye.
[*Barelle kisses him, then turns to the King*]

BARELLE

Be quiet now and follow.
Be careful.

THE KING

I'll be careful. I know how.

ROBERT

Good-bye.

ANTOINE

O shut your mouth!
[*With a sudden blow he knocks Robert to the floor*]

THE KING

[*Standing stock still*]
I cannot go.

I had not thought of that.—I cannot go.
    You are too little.

JEANNE
        I 'll be here.   I'll take
His part.

THE KING
            You can't, you can't, when Master—
    No!

ANTOINE
    Go while the going's good.   You're wasting
        time.
    [*Antoine lurches out and is heard calling*]
    I've found the brandy, Friend.   She tried
        to hide it.

THE KING
    O no, Robert! the people over there,
    If they should find me gone, would punish
        you
    And maybe kill you.

ROBERT
    [*Rising*]
            But they won't find out.

I'll turn my head away and I won't talk
To them.

THE KING

He'll make you talk. He'll make
you sing.
And when he has you here alone, Robert——!
I had not thought of that. I cannot go.

BARELLE

They'll soon find out who Robert is——

JEANNE

What's this?

BARELLE

They'll think that he was used
will,
Without his knowing,—and th
him go.

THE KING

Once you are here, they never let
O no, Robert, give me my coat,
[*He slips off Robert's coat*]

JEANNE

You little chump, keep on that coat! Behave
Yourself! You're stubborn as your mother.

THE KING

Am I?

ROBERT

Please, little King, please, please!

RELLE

Your Majesty!

KING

*Barelle's attempts to put the coat
im*]

go. You cannot make me go.
could never stand it as I can.
can stand—O more than anyone!

old him, Citizen. Bring him your

Come now, Capet, behave your-

THE KING

[*Still resisting the coat, and throwing the cap down*]

And then, besides, I've thought of something else.

You might save me and not my Mother-Queen.

She might be left here all alone upstairs.

JEANNE

She's not upstairs, you little whining fool.

They should have killed you too and saved us trouble,

You with your mother, the whelp with the she-wolf!

BARELLE

O shame!

THE KING

My Mother-Queen?

JEANNE

To-day at noon.

You heard the bells, Capet, and drank her health!

BARELLE
  Great God!

ROBERT
  [*Taking the other boy's hand*]
        Poor little King!

THE KING
        It is not true.
  You wish to make me go.   It is not true.
  If it were true, you would have told me then.
  I will not go and leave my Mother-Queen.
  I will not go.

JEANNE
        Tell him it's true and get
  Him out of here.   We haven't time to fool
  Away like this.

BARELLE
  [*Tenderly, gravely*]
        Your Majesty, it's true.

THE KING
  My Mama-Queen?

BARELLE

      Is with your father, Sire.
She died to-day, as brave as she had lived.
They would not let her say good-bye to you.

ROBERT
  Poor little King!

THE KING
  [*With a sob*]
      She isn't dead! no, no,
She isn't dead.   My Mama isn't dead.

BARELLE
  Be brave, your Majesty, as she was brave.
A man on horseback told me what she said.
She said: 'I was a Queen and you de-
    throned me.
I was a wife and you have killed my husband.
I was a mother and you tear my children
Away from me.   Only my blood is left.
Make haste to shed it.   And be satisfied.'

THE KING
  O she was brave, my Mother, wasn't she!
I'm going to be like Mother.

ROBERT
>   Little King!

BARELLE
>   Then, don't you see, you owe it to your
>   kingdom
>   And to her memory to come with me?
>   That will be brave, your Majesty.

JEANNE
>   Go on,
>   Flatter him up!   Perhaps he'll take to that.
>   I never saw such people as these Capets.

BARELLE
>   And you shall have your sword again and
>   come
>   Some day to punish murderers.

THE KING
>   O sir,
>   I promised both my Father and my Mother
>   Never to hurt the people.   But I'm not
>   Afraid of them.   My Father said to me
>   He could not run away from them and be
>   A coward.   That was why we all came back.

And I should be ashamed to run away
And not be like my Father and my Mother.

JEANNE
Shut up his talk! Get busy while there's
time!
Take him!
[Barelle and Jeanne Marie try again to
force Robert's jacket on the King, who strug-
gles against them]

THE KING
No, you shall not.

BARELLE
[Passionately]
Your Majesty!
[They lead him into the anteroom, the King
contesting every inch of the way]

BARELLE
For God's sake!

JEANNE
Little fool!

THE KING
I will not go.

BARELLE

If you betray us, it will be the end.

THE KING

O won't you please obey me? Won't you
please?—
[*He breaks away. Barelle follows and lays
hold of him again. But, with a sudden royal
gesture, he checks Barelle in the centre of
the room*]
I am the King of France. Obey me, sir,
And take your hands away.

BARELLE

God's will be done.

JEANNE

[*Trying to pass Barelle*]
God's nothing! It's the antic of a child!
[*Barelle holds Jeanne Marie back while the
King helps Robert into the washerboy's coat*]

THE KING

But O be sure, be sure you come again!
The Simons will not dare to tell on you,

For I should tell on them. Take all the
  clothes!
[*Picking up Jeanne Marie's bundle from the
table*]
Take these as well, Robert. And look inside
And you will find a keepsake there from me.

JEANNE
Not on your life!

THE KING
        You wish me then to tell?
[*Jeanne Marie stands back glowering while
he gives Robert the bundle. Then he takes
the lily from his bouquet and hands it to
Barelle*]
This lily is much better than the pear.

BARELLE
I ask you, Sire, to let her keep the money.
She would be kinder.

THE KING
        Take them all, Robert.
[*Barelle bows and hides the lily in his
breast*]

JEANNE

You little cur—you devil out of hell!
[*Hearing the stairs creak*]
The officer!
[*Barelle crosses to the window and seals the next to the last opening*]

ANTOINE

[*Entering, at the big door, heavy with brandy, his finger on his lips*]
He's on his way downstairs.

BARELLE

It does not matter now. My work is done.

ANTOINE

[*Looking closely at Robert*]
Your work is done, you say? What do you mean?

BARELLE

All but one stone.

ANTOINE

One stone?

THE KING

      Good-bye, my friends.

*[Barelle kneels and kisses the King's hand.
The King will not let Robert kneel, but puts
an arm about him and kisses him on the
lips. Robert goes out with the basket at the
big door]*

BARELLE

Surely you cannot punish him for this!
What has he done but shown that tyranny
May go by any name and wear red caps,—
While loving comradeship may dwell in
    kings!—
Father, forget not he's a little boy!

*[Jeanne Marie hurries Barelle out and closes
the door after him]*

JEANNE

He wouldn't go.

ANTOINE

      You rotten little snake!

JEANNE

He gave the money back. He said he'd tell.

THE KING
You cannot buy and sell the King of France.

ANTOINE
But we can make him pay!
[*He goes to the cage of canaries and starts
to bring a chair down over it*]

THE KING
[*In the way*]
        What are you doing?

ANTOINE
I'm smashing up your royal bird that pipes
' The March of the King. '

THE KING
        But not the other birds!
O not the one——!

ANTOINE
        Which one?

THE KING
        —that sings to us!
The little one!   The ribbon's on his neck!

ANTOINE
> So that's your toy!—your kingdom in a
> cage!
> And orders, marks! We'll see!

THE KING
>   The ribbon's red!—
> He's my republican canary, Master!

ANTOINE
> Favorite of the King, come out here, you!
> [*He thrusts his hand into the cage and takes
> out the bird*]

THE KING
> O give him, give him to me!

ANTOINE
>   There he is.
> [*He wrings the bird's neck and throws its
> dead body on the floor*]

THE KING
> [*Kneeling and taking the bird up tenderly*]
> O listen to me, please, dear Heavenly
> Father!

JEANNE
Don't mention God again!—There is no
God.

THE KING
—Help me to be as brave as Mother was.

ANTOINE
Get up.   Give that to me.   Here, Jeanne
Marie,
[*Taking the bird from the King, he tosses
it to her*]
Cook it for supper.
[*He jerks the King to his feet and points
to the red cap on the floor*]
        Now pick up that cap!

JEANNE
And put it on again!
[*The King faces them, not moving*]

ANTOINE
        You dirty pup!

JEANNE
You put that on!—or else we'll punish you

Worse than you've ever dreamed. The
    window's sealed,
Capet.   And now we'll seal this door, and
    this,
And cut a little hole here in the middle,
And then hand in your food to you and leave
    you.
Alone in the dark, all day, all night, forever.
You've heard the rats here in the walls?
    They'll all
Come out, when you can't see them, and
    they'll eat
Your food.   And then they'll eat your fin-
    gers, Capet.
And bugs and worms and snakes will come
    and wait
For you to go to sleep.—Pick up that cap.

ANTOINE
    Pick up that cap.
    [*The King moves toward it and quietly
    stands on it, facing them.   Antoine crosses
    and sets the last stone in the window, darken-
    ing the stage so that only shadows are seen*]

JEANNE
    [*Pointing, trying to laugh*]

Behold the little King!
[*Then they open the big door and close it behind them, and leave him standing in the darkness*]

CURTAIN

A NIGHT WIND

To Edna St. Vincent Millay

[*Heard coming up the dark stairs, and
pausing in the door at the back, a young
Poet enters The Pyramid, a dingy huddled
half-lighted coffee-room in Greenwich Vil-
lage. At the left, from behind a screen,
which partly hides a stove and shelves
cluttered with pots and pans, appears ear-
ringed Egypt, draped in a brightly em-
broidered shawl, an Alexandrian with
deep quick eyes. She stands against the
screen and nods to the poet, who crosses
and sits near her on a bench beside one of
the long low rough tables of smoky wood.
He gazes at her, silent*]

EGYPT.

    [*In a warm husky voice*]
Why do you look?

THE POET.

Your eyes.

EGYPT.

What do you find?

THE POET.
You have had secrets, Egypt.

EGYPT.

So have you.

THE POET.
But I tell all mine.

EGYPT.

O, what a foolish poet!
You should almost tell them.   People listen
    then,
Hoping to hear the secret.   If I told,
Would anybody listen any more?
Secrets are what they buy here with their
    coffee,
Shadows of secrets.   After all, my friend,
Secrets themselves are not mysterious,
Only their shadows.

THE POET.

                   Such as death, for instance.
Death makes of life a secret worth the
    solving.
Perhaps if we could solve it, see beyond,
Life would be something to avoid at once.
I'm a philosopher, Egypt.   But I'm human.
I want the thing I know I shouldn't want.
You're much more wonderful, just as you
    are,
Than if the desert-cat explained herself.
But I want to see one of the shadows move,
A falling fragment of the pyramid.

EGYPT.

Life is the pyramid, with death inside.

THE POET.

Let's have a bit of the surface then.   Come
    on!
One of your secrets, Egypt, one of your
    loves,
And I'll have some coffee too and a couple of
    cakes.

EGYPT.
 Which cake?

THE POET.
             The dark one with the honey in it.

EGYPT.
 And the secret with the honey in it?

THE POET.
                                Yes.
 Abdul, for instance.

EGYPT.
 [*Smiling and crossing for the coffee*]
                Abdul is no secret.
 Abdul's the evening paper—of last year.
 I read him, though.   The news is never new.

THE POET.
 Never?

EGYPT.
        Well, almost never.   Once, just once.
 Only one secret.

THE POET.

Who was yours?
[*Egypt returns with the coffee and cakes and, as she sets them down, whispers in his ear*]

THE POET.

Not really?
I haven't seen him round here for some time. Where has he been?

EGYPT.

The coast—with Muriel.

THE POET.

Oh?

EGYPT.
But he's back.

THE POET.

And she?

EGYPT.

She's back.   Richer than ever.

Her mother died. And Muriel gave a
  party,
Everything gray and green and lavender
To go with absinthe from the family-cellar.
  [*Handing him a clipping which she unpins
  from the wall*]
The San Francisco paper told about it.
He arrived in town this morning. He'll be
  round.
He'll come to The Pyramid and drink his
  coffee
And never speak.

THE POET.
                    And she?

EGYPT.
                    She used to come—
With her furs. Not any more, I don't know
  why.
Perhaps I do. I hope to God I do.

THE POET.
  Does Abdul know?

EGYPT.

         He knows as much as I know.
I tell him everything I have to tell.
I take off all my shadows.   He's a bathtub.
I bathe in him.

THE POET.

         And in the other one?

EGYPT.
  In him, you mean?

THE POET.

         Your secret.

EGYPT.

            Don't you laugh.
  I used to swim.
    [*A Girl enters, with bobbed hair and a
    surface hardness, handsome tall and
    strong, yet haggard and nervous*]

THE GIRL.

         Give me some coffee, Egypt.

EGYPT.
  You left your flask at home?

THE GIRL.

                    I got to quit.

THE POET.
  What's up?

THE GIRL.
        I got to sleep.

THE POET.

                On coffee?

THE GIRL.

                    Sure.
  Coffee's my good-night kiss.   And here's my
      dreams.
    [*Taking out of her smock a phial of tab-
    lets and pouring some of them out on the
    table*]
  The doctor gave 'em to me.   One of 'em,
  Not more than one, he said.   But, Lord,
  I guess I must 'a' got a pickled heart!

Four do the job for me.   I tried first one,
Then two, then three.   But four's my num-
     ber, kid.
I slept last night.
     [*A Fellow comes into the room, with a
     heavy, surly magnetism*]
               What do you know!   He's back!
You never answered my letter, did you!

THE FELLOW.

                                        No.
     [*Egypt takes a hesitant step toward him.
     He nods to her and to the poet.   She
     crosses to the stove and returns with two
     cups of coffee, which she places on the
     table.   He starts again toward the door*]

EGYPT.
  You're leaving?

THE FELLOW.
               Telephone.

THE GIRL.

                    To Muriel?

THE FELLOW.

                              Yes.

THE GIRL.
  You got a date?

THE FELLOW.
            I have.   In half an hour.   *Everf-boy*
  [*He goes out. Egypt returns to the
  stove*]

THE GIRL.
  I thought they were out west.

THE POET.
  [*Handing her the clipping from the table*]
                              They were.

THE GIRL.
  [*Reading*]

                              Some baby!
  Has to keep going, doesn't she!

THE POET.

                              Good-looking,

Knows what she wants and takes it too,
   that's all.

THE GIRL.

She knows what other people want, that's
   all—
Takes it away from 'em for fun, that's all,
Buys it whether she wants it or not, that's
   all—
To spite 'em, that's her way. I'll fix her
   party,
I'll give him one o' these and make him
   sleepy.

THE POET.

That's not a bad idea.

THE GIRL.

                      You're right, it isn't.
Here goes for mine.
   [*She drops four tablets into her coffee*]

EGYPT.

   [*From the screen*]
                  Doesn't it spoil the taste?

THE GIRL.
No taste at all.

EGYPT.
To the coffee?

THE GIRL.
To the stuff.
[*Egypt goes behind the screen again*]

THE GIRL.
[*Continuing to the poet*]
And as for him, he's worse'n Muriel is,—
A great big husky, playing off he's sick,
Pretending that his heart is on the bum,
Making us mother him, us damn fool women.
Why is it women like to be damn fools?
Got to have something. Guess I'll buy a
dog—
And no more soul-stuff!

THE POET.
So he talks.

THE GIRL.

You bet
He's glum enough, with other people round—
But when he's alone with a girl, he talks his
    head off.
The line o' soul-stuff he can pull, my God!
Give me an animal that knows he's one.
*[She drinks her coffee, while the poet
crosses to the screen and, with his hand on
its top, speaks beyond it. Egypt's face is
visible over the screen]*

THE POET.
There's a night-wind on the desert. Some-
    thing moves—
A fragment falling from the pyramid,
The shadow of a secret.

EGYPT.

Let it fall.
*[They do not notice the girl slipping four
of her tablets into the fellow's cup]*

THE POET.
Two shadows, Egypt.

EGYPT.

                    Yes?

THE POET.

                              One secret, Egypt.

EGYPT.

   You poets know too much.
   [*She comes to the table with her own
   coffee*]

THE POET.

                    We know too much—
   Yes, about everything except ourselves.
   [*The fellow comes back again. Egypt indicates his cup. He sits with head and
   shoulders forward, his hat shading his
   face. They all drink their coffee, except
   Egypt, who watches him*]

THE POET.
   How soon does it make you sleepy?

THE GIRL.

                              Right away,
   With four of 'em.

THE POET.

What about his?

THE GIRL.

No go.
Let 'em alone.   It's a free world, I say.
Each to his taste, however bad it is!
   [*Rising dully*]
Good-night.   It's me for bed.

THE POET.

Sleep well.

THE GIRL.

You bet.
   [*She goes out.   The poet picks up the
   clipping again*]

THE POET.
   [*To the fellow*]
I see that you and Muriel made a hit
In San Francisco with your absinthe party.
A drink out there's like christening a ship,

Breaking a bottle on the prow of the world.
Didn't it strike you that way?

THE FELLOW.

No.

THE POET.

I'm sorry.

I'll look in later, Egypt.
    [*Egypt nods and the poet leaves them.
    There is a pause*]

EGYPT.

Why do you come?
You always come like this.   And you never
    speak.
 Do you care for Muriel?   For anyone? . . .
I am going to tell you something.   All this
    time
I have let you come.   You can't come any
    more. ──
It's them or me.   It can't be all of us.
Here's what I've got to say.   I've gone
    along,
I've tried it out the way you told me to.

No use, there's nothing in it.   You're my
    man.

But we got to be clean, we got to be straight
    with ourselves,

We got to take each other or let go.

You always think there's something round
    the corner.

I used to think so too.   But, after all,

Soon as you're round the corner, it's the
    same—

There's something round another corner,
    see?

And here's the truth of it, here's the whole
    thing—

There's something round the corner, looking
    back,

Something that's just as good, the thing you
    had,

Something that's better if you'll only take it

And not be restless, not be on the hunt,

Looking for something you can never
    find . . .

Go out and ask the sky, all by yourself . . .

If it's a home you had—honest-to-God

Real home, I mean—you'd better turn around

And choose the thing you know you got.
 Speak up
And tell me now. Do you want this home
 in here?
 [*She presses both her hands to her heart*]
It's here. You can count on that, it's here.
 And mine—
Is there—with you, old boy.
 [*She clasps his hand on the table*]
  What makes your hand—?
What makes it cold! You're cold, you're
 icy cold!
 [*His arms had supported his weight. As
 she picks up his two hands, his body falls
 forward. She lifts him up. His head
 topples back and his hat off, revealing
 a face dead-white and lifeless. After a
 moment, she is sure. She lets his shoulders rest again on the table, just as the
 girl enters breathless at the door.*]

THE GIRL.
 Has he drunk it? I was a fool! He
  mustn't drink it!

All right for me, but I forgot his heart!
I put 'em in his coffee, four of 'em.
    [*Knowing by the look in Egypt's face*]
I killed him, Egypt, but I didn't mean to!

EGYPT.
I wonder if he's thinking anything.

THE GIRL.
And Muriel waiting for him.

EGYPT.

                              So was I.

    [*The poet enters*]

THE GIRL.
He's dead.   I killed him.

THE POET.

                    Not with the tablets!

THE GIRL.

                                        Yes.

THE POET.
    [*Appalled*]
It will be all right.

EGYPT.

It will be all right for him.

THE POET.
  [*Putting the fellow's cup into his own
  pocket*]
  It was his heart.   I saw him.   I was here.
  It was his heart.

EGYPT.

Take her away, my friend.

THE POET.
  What else can I do?

EGYPT.

Call up the coroner.

THE POET.
  I'll try to. But it's late—

EGYPT.

I understand.
  They'll come here in the morning.   That's
  all right.

THE POET.

But there's no one with you, Egypt.

EGYPT.

Yes, there is.

[*The poet leads out the dazed girl. Egypt closes the door behind them and locks it*]

EGYPT.

[*Returning to him*]

—Have you decided to come home, my dear? [*She takes off her bright-colored shawl, covers the figure with it, then sits beside him*]

CURTAIN

TIGER

To Arthur Davison Ficke

'*Tiger, tiger, burning bright*
In the forests of the night,
What immortal hand or eye
Could frame thy fearful symmetry?'

Time: Evening.

Scene: A room in a house not far east of Times Square. A curtained door at the back of the stage leads into the hallway. A closed door at the right leads into an inner bedroom. The furniture and pictures are more showy than expensive. The shades are drawn.

At the rise of the curtain, the keeper of the house sits in an easy-chair. She is a woman of thirty-five, handsome, well-dressed. Her familiars call her Tiger, on account of her hard, lithe brilliance. She is looking over a handful of bills and writing cheques with a fountain-pen on the arm of the chair. On a couch reclines Annabel, a girl of twenty-four, beginning to fade under her paint, but an effective type still, with her hair parted and drawn simply over her forehead to a flat coil behind.

*She is in a loose, thin dressing-gown, reading
a novel, eating chocolates and smoking cigarettes.   An ash-tray, cigarettes, chewing-gum
and the chocolates are on a chair beside the
couch.   At a table across the room, a man of
thirty, with somewhat refined features, a sug-
gestive pallor and flush, and a habit of biting
the skin on his red lips and of rubbing his
thumb over his finger-tips, is pouring himself
a glass of straight gin.   He is over-dressed,
over-mannered and wears several bright rings,
but might pass with the young for a gentleman.
On account of what is known as his 'class,' he
has been dubbed The Baron.*

ANNABEL.
   Put water in it, Baron.   Spare your liver.

BARON.
   Mind your own liver and shut up, will you?
Whenever I want your dope, I'll ask for it.
   [*She returns to her reading.   He gulps
   his drink, then loiters toward Tiger.   Suddenly he sits on the arm of her chair,
   catches her close and kisses her hard*]

TIGER.

   [*Pushing him away*]
Cut out that stuff, Baron.
   [*Picking up her bills from the floor*]
                     Come across first
With what you promised.

BARON.

                  Oh, you needn't worry,
Dear Mama Shylock. You're going to
   get your pound
Of flesh,—I've said that you shall have her
   here
To-night. She may be waiting for me now—
   [*He looks at his wrist-watch*]
Less than a block away, ready to serve
And honor and obey me.—Damn you,
   Tiger!
I wonder if I love you more or hate you.
Damn you, anyway!

TIGER.

               Oh, swear your head off!
Go over it again, make up your mind
One way and then the other!

[*Looking up from her bills*]

Kiss me, kid!

[*He kisses her hungrily. She stands up
and throws him away from her*]

Now snarl at me, you cur. I don't know
    why

I keep you round; except to purr and snarl

Myself,—first kiss your feminine eyes
    because

They look so lost in the world, then curse
    your breed,

You most of all, because you're so unlike

The brutes I'm tired of.

[*She crosses to lay bills and cheques in
her desk*]

But what's the use

Of bothering? You suit me. And you're
    good

For the business. Run along and bring her
    here.

[*She sits at her desk and writes*]

BARON.

Remember now. She's young, and I'm her
    first

Offence. And I've been careful with her,
    Tiger,
Not touched her fingers only once or twice
And used good English and been sym-
    pathetic.

TIGER.
Oh, yes, I know all that.

BARON.
    [*Taking a cigarette from Annabel's
    supply*]
                    She's different though,
She hasn't got the taste for it beforehand
Most of them have.

TIGER.
    [*Looking round as she seals a letter*]
                    Then she's the very kind
We want, old boy. The other kind is com-
    mon
And some of our customers amuse them-
    selves,
You know, by being fastidious. Is she a
    blonde?

BARON.
Brunette.

TIGER.

Worse luck.
BARON.

No, you can fix that up.
Light hair'd go fine with her dark eyes, good
    change.
She's just the girl for it, solemn and slow
And innocent.   Poor kid, I pity her.

TIGER.
You act like you were getting stuck on her;
Perhaps she'll keep you when you're tired
    of me.

BARON.
You've got me hypnotized. I don't get tired.

TIGER.
[*She approaches him, seductively, mock-
    ingly*]
Be true to me, sweetheart!

BARON.

> To hell with you!

[*She lays her hand insidiously on his arm. At once he seizes and kisses her. She leads him to the hallway door, and opens it as he kisses her again, then she pushes him out with both hands and, closing the door, turns back to Annabel, who at every amorous passage between Tiger and the Baron has looked up from her book and watched with curious but accustomed interest*]

ANNABEL.

[*Chewing gum*]
Gee, but I wish I had a man like that!

TIGER.

You'd have one, dear, if you were business-like.

ANNABEL.

[*Shaking her head and marking her place in the book with a cigarette*]
I couldn't hold a man. They get so bored
With me. And, after all, there isn't much

To say to one man.   I'd be bored myself
To have to think of new things all the time.
Variety, Tiger, is the spice of life,
Not in the spiel but in the spielers.   Dear,
Do you like my hair this way?   One of the
        boys
Suggested that it makes me look too old.
I think I'll put it back again.
    [*She starts to uncoil it*]

TIGER.

                              No, no!
Leave it to me!   You'll be told quick enough
When you look old.   Let it alone.

ANNABEL.

                              Well, looks
Ain't everything.   I'm getting wise to the
        game.
Say to a gink, 'Your nose is beautiful,'
'Your mouth was made to kiss,' or call his
        figure
Military.
    [*She examines herself critically in a hand-
    mirror which she takes from under a sofa-
    cushion*]

TIGER.

There's just one kind of figure
That makes a hit with me.   A good full
chest!

ANNABEL.

Gee, ain't they handsome when they have
green—backs!
[*They laugh*]
I told a guy last night that it takes dough
To make a tart.   Dear, that's my own!

TIGER.

And say,
Here's business, Annabel, take it from me!
You've seen the belly on the dollar-sign?—
Well, the man who has the stomach has the
figure!

ANNABEL.

I've noticed that.

TIGER.

Sure thing!   And while he thinks

You're waiting for his phoney kisses—pay
Attention to his stomach and his roll!
Make him eat, drink and spend!   My dear,
    the way
To passion's thro' the stomach every time.

ANNABEL.
    [*Meditative*]
Champagne, you mean?

TIGER.

               Eve got there with an apple.
But the apple has fermented some since then.

ANNABEL.
    [*Laughing with Tiger*]
We have a good time, don't we!

TIGER

                  You do, dear.
You've been here seven months and,
    Annabel,
You never once in all that time have had
A grouch.

ANNABEL.

You're square with me, Tiger, that's
why.

TIGER.

But, on the level, you don't like the life?

ANNABEL.

Better than selling underwear to women
And paying fines on four whole bucks a
week!
Talk as you please, the men have more
respect
For a girl that's a good looker and can earn
A seat in a restaurant than for a dub
Who stands up all day waiting on their
wives.

TIGER.

Besides, you have as good a chance as me
To save up coin enough before you're old
And rent a house and get some girls to-
gether—
And after a while to live in a good hotel

And settle down respectable.—Perhaps
A friend or two.   But independent.

ANNABEL.

                                    Chance!
Yes, I've got that.   But, dear, I haven't got
The brains to make a hit in any line.
I know my limit and I'm satisfied.
I'm better off than I ever was at home,
And that's enough.   The future can go hang.
There's more than one way to prepare a
        corpse.
Ain't I the cheerful guy?

TIGER.

                            You're lazy, dear,
That's all the matter with you.

ANNABEL.

                            Who's the new girl?

TIGER.

Oh, I don't know,   The Baron falls for me
So I can trust his taste.

ANNABEL.

                            Say, does he fall?
He's jealous, now, of me!

TIGER.

Who's on the job

Downstairs?

ANNABEL.

Cassie to-night. I'm tired. She knows
The steps and laughs a lot, loosens 'em up.
She's popular.

TIGER.

And she's the Baron's work,—
He brought her here last winter. Cassie
thinks
The Baron the one bet and he, poor kid,
Just keeps her on because I tell him to.
And see how well the combination works?—
The happy family!

ANNABEL.

Business-like's the word!

[*A knock is heard at the hallway door*]

TIGER.

Quick there! Be business-like yourself for
once!
Clear off those things!

ANNABEL.

All right.

[*While Annabel puts bottles and glasses under the table so that they are hidden by the table-cover, Tiger picks up the gum, cigarettes and ash-tray from the chair and tucks them all under a sofa-cushion. The knock is repeated*]

ANNABEL.

My fancy-work,
Where is it?

TIGER.

[*Taking a piece of embroidery from under a cushion*]
Here.
[*She hands it to Annabel and crosses to the easy chair*]

ANNABEL.

[*Sitting on the couch, with the embroidery, as though she had been sewing*]
Now we're a boarding-house!

TIGER.

Throw me the book!

[*Annabel throws Tiger the novel from
the couch, Tiger holds it as though she
had been reading*]

Come in!

[*The Baron enters, leading by the hand
Margaret, a simple, romantic girl of
sixteen. She is in street-clothes. She
looks toward the two women bashfully,
innocently, as they rise and come toward
her*]

BARON.

It's Margaret.
This is Miss Dillingham, my aunt, and
     here's
My Cousin Ann.

MARGARET.

How do you do? Gene's told
Me lots about you.   I suppose you think
I'm foolish running away like this?

TIGER.

                                        Why, no!
You loved each other, Margaret.

MARGARET.

                                        My aunt
Was angry when he wanted to call. You
    see,
She's not like you, Miss Dillingham; she's
    set
And so old-fashioned. And she thought be-
    cause
Gene works in a store he isn't good enough.
She said I never should have talked with
    him
At all. And then she didn't like his voice
On the telephone. . . . I do, don't I,
    Eugene!

BARON.
    [*His arm round her*]
I guess you do, darling.

MARGARET.

                            You see, my aunt
Has been with us for years and father takes

Her word as law. I knew what she would
    say
About Eugene and how she'd make it sound.
At first I thought he'd better go himself
And see my father.

BARON.

                    But I told you, dear,
He wouldn't fall for me. And give you
    up?
I couldn't, could I!

MARGARET.

                    No. And so I thought
And thought—and prayed. And finally I
    came.

TIGER.

    And aren't you tired out? Let Annabel
Show you your room. You ought to rest
    before
Your marriage, dear.
    [*Annabel opens the bedroom door. Mar-
    garet, vaguely troubled, does not follow
    her*]

MARGARET.

We must be married now.

BARON.
  To-morrow.

MARGARET.

Oh, I thought to-night.

BARON.

But first
I have to get a license and attend
To things like that. And I can leave you
    here
With Tige—Miss Dillingham. She'll take
    good care
Of you.

MARGARET.
  [*Doubtfully*]
      I'll do, Gene, as you say.

ANNABEL.

Your room
  Is ready for you.

MARGARET.
  [*Crossing to the Baron*]
                    If I'd only waited
And told my father! He might not have
    felt
As Aunt Louisa felt. It seems so mean
Of me to run away from him. But I left
A little message on his dressing-case
Saying that he would hear from me to-
    morrow.

TIGER.
  You didn't write him anything about
  Eugene?—or where you——

MARGARET.
                    We thought best to wait,
  Not to say anything till we could go
  Together, to him, married, hand in hand,
  And make him like us both.

TIGER.
                    When will he find
  The note?

MARGARET.

>   To-night.   Or—let me see,—
>   what day—?
> Why, it's Friday!   Then he won't be home
>   till Monday.
> I hadn't thought of that.   He always goes
> To the country somewhere Sunday with his
>   friends.
> Poor Aunt Louisa will be scared to death
> When I'm not back for dinner.

ANNABEL.

>   But the note.
> She'll find it.

BARON.

>   Sure, and send your father word.

MARGARET.
> She won't know where to reach him.

ANNABEL.

>   Then I'll go
> And 'phone your auntie that you're safe
>   with me,—
> One of your friends.   Who shall I say I am?

MARGARET.
  Oh no, that would be worse.

TIGER.
                          That would be lying.
  You must be tired, Margaret.

MARGARET.
                          Yes, I am.
    [*With a smile*]
  You see, I never ran away before.

ANNABEL.
  Didn't you bring——?

MARGARET.
                      I didn't dare. I just
  Went out and walked like some one in a
      dream
  And took the train. My heart was beat-
      ing so,
  I thought that people would look round
      at me.

TIGER.
  And did they?

MARGARET.

          No.

TIGER.

                  That's right! Come,
    Annabel,
She's talked enough for now. Lend her
    something
To wear to-night.

ANNABEL.

        Sure will I.
    [*As she goes up toward the hallway door,
    a knock is heard*]
                  Who's there?
    [*She opens the door slightly and takes
    from some one a cup of tea*]
                      Thanks.

TIGER.

    [*Crossing and taking the cup from
    Annabel*]
Oh, yes, we've made some nice, hot tea.
    [*Exit Annabel*]

MARGARET.

For me?

No, thanks.

TIGER.

Take it this once, it'll do you good.

MARGARET.

[*Tasting it*]

Isn't it very strong?

TIGER.

There's medicine——

MARGARET.

I don't need medicine.

TIGER.

It's very little.

Only to rest your nerves and make you sleep.

MARGARET.

[*To the Baron*]

I'll take it if you ask me.

BARON.

Take it, dear.

That's right. All down!

MARGARET.

It burns.

BARON.

One
swallow more!
[*Annabel returns with a night-dress*]

TIGER.

Leave her to Ann and me now till the
morning.

BARON.

There.   Thank you, sweetheart.
[*He takes the empty cup from her and
hands it to Tiger, who lays it down*]
Good-night,
Margaret.
[*He holds her hand in both his*]

MARGARET.

Good-night, Eugene.
[*She shyly lifts her face to him. He kisses
her*]

BARON.

>To-morrow, darling!

MARGARET.

>Yes.

[*Margaret goes into the bedroom. Annabel, with a wink to the others, follows her, closing the door. The Baron turns from Margaret and looks at Tiger, who stands facing him with her arms down. She smiles and nods. He crosses to her, puts his arms round her, holds her now with assurance and kisses her. She responds by kissing his eyes.*

The stage now darkens to indicate the lapse of time from Friday night to Sunday night. When it grows light again, a small table is beside the couch, with a chair or two round it, and with cards on it and poker-chips. The Baron sits on the couch idly throwing poker-dice. Annabel, who has been as idly watching him, crosses to the closed door of the bedroom and leans with her ear to the crack of it]

ANNABEL.

>[*Moving away again from the door*]
>That little girl's more bother than she's
>worth.

BARON.

>[*Still throwing the dice*]
>The stuff you gave her in that tea started
>The devil in her. Every finger-nail
>In action! Tiger bawled me out for quitting.
>Poor little girl! I wish she wasn't caught.
>Damn it, I was a dog!

ANNABEL.

>   Well, you lap the hand
>That feeds you!

BARON.

>[*Putting down the dice*]
>   Shut up now! I can know myself
>And kick myself.   But I won't let you do it!

ANNABEL.

>Oh, well, who wants to kick a rotten egg?

BARON.

> [*He jumps up and, catching her by the wrist, twists it*]

I'll teach you——

ANNABEL.

> [*Catching him in the stomach with her knee*]

Will you?

> [*Tiger enters from the hallway*]

TIGER.

Stop making love, you two!

> [*Crossing and listening at the door*]

How is she, quiet?

ANNABEL.

There hasn't been a squeak To-day.

BARON.

> [*Back at his dice*]

My God, she couldn't cry any more!

[*Tiger turns round at his tone, crosses to him, lifts his chin with her fingers and looks into his eyes*]

TIGER

If you should dare to let her out, you fool!

BARON.

Who's going to let her out? I did the thing. And I know why. And you know why I did it!

TIGER.

[*Walking away from him*]

I've paid you.

BARON.

[*Amorous*]

Kiss me, Tige!

TIGER.

Let me alone!

[*Turning sharply*]

Good God, you don't think I'm in this for fun!

I'm in it for the future. And there'll be No Baron in my future.

[*She walks away again*]

BARON.

[*He follows her and, grasping her shoulders, turns her to face him*]

Wait and see!

You'll need me, Tiger, more than I'll need you.

TIGER.

[*Looking at him shrewdly*]

You think so? Annabel, bring me her clothes.

I guess I'll keep an eye on them myself.

[*Exit Annabel into the hall*]

BARON.

There's mighty little you don't keep an eye on.

TIGER.

You nearly took up Cassie for your girl,

And Cassie bores you, Baron. Some one's got

To use their eyes for you. You don't use yours.

BARON.

You're jealous, Tige.   Insult me, kid, I
love it!

TIGER.

It's business, Baron.   Jealousy's a joke.
You know me well enough to quit your bluff
And quit me too, or else to give this girl
The go-by.   It's plain business.   Do you get
me?

ANNABEL.

[*Returning with Margaret's clothes and
hat*]

Where shall I put them, Tiger?

TIGER.

Leave them there
For now.   And put that over them.

[*She indicates her own cloak.   Annabel
lays them on the couch*]

BARON.

[*Cowed*]

You're dippy.
I wouldn't do a thing you didn't want.

TIGER.

[*Crossing toward the bedroom*]
What time is it? I guess I'll try again.

BARON.
She hasn't had a bite of food—since when?

ANNABEL.
Not since she came.

BARON.
Lord, Tiger, give her something!

TIGER.
This is my business now. You've done your
part.
Get out of here!

BARON.
You bet!

TIGER.
Come back on Tuesday.
These little cooings will be over then.

BARON.

> They're over now.   I love you, Tige, you
>> devil!
> [*He kisses her passionately*]

TIGER.

> [*Wearily*]
> Good-night.

> [*Exit the Baron*]

ANNABEL.

> You sure have got him going, Tiger.

TIGER.

> I'm sick of him!   But I can't throw him
>> down.
> The fool might shoot me or else go and blab.
> He's the only one I've cared for in ten years;
> And I knew, the night I met him, that I ought
> To look away and leave him be.   It comes
> Of letting sentiment into your business.

ANNABEL.

> I wonder if I'll ever fall in love.

TIGER.
    The only other man I ever loved
    Married me, and he used me like a dog.
    The time I wasted moping for that boy
    Would have set me up by now in Easy
        Street.
    I hung on fourteen months.   He didn't hand
    Me coin enough for food—there were other
        girls
    More business-like who hadn't married
        him—
    Then he cussed me when I couldn't buy his
        friends
    Big eats at home.   One of them helped me
        out
    The last two months.   He liked me.   And
        I ran
    Away with him.   I learned a lot from him.
    A man's an easy mark unless you love him.
    I love that first one yet.

    [*Crossing to the bedroom door and signi-
    fying Margaret with her head*]
                  She loves the Baron.

    [*Speaking through the door*]

Margaret?—When you choose you can have
    food.

Just say the word and you'll have it—not
    before.

You know what good your screams did
    yesterday!—

And you can cry till doomsday if you want,

Nobody'll hear. Your father'll never come.

And you won't kill yourself. I didn't, dear.

Just say the word, I'll send you in Eugene—

Or some one else—and food!

ANNABEL.

> [*Improving her make-up. Pallor and red
> lips are effective with her black hair*]
>   She may be dead.

TIGER.

Dead nothing! I can hear her through the
    door.

She'll come to terms. Hunger and time are
    good

Persuaders. And she knows the Baron's
    waiting.

He'll teach her first. Then nothing mat-
    ters much.

Ten or twelve hours more and she'll begin.
She'll not be too unhappy, *you* know that,—
Probably happier than she would have been
With a cold husband and an empty life
Selected for her by her Aunt Louisa.

[*There's a knock at the hallway door.
Annabel goes to it*]

TIGER.
Who is it?

ANNABEL.
Willie's here.
TIGER.
Well, let him in.
ANNABEL.
You think——?

TIGER.
It's safe enough. He's an old friend.
He knows the game and plays it like a good
one.
In fact it's sports like Willie have to have
The dainty morsels.

[*She moves Annabel out of the way and
opens the door herself*]

Come in. How are things?

[*Enter Willie, a patron, of later middle-
age, a stout, prosperous-looking, pleasant
gentleman*]

WILLIE.

I'm fine—but hungry, Tiger. Cassie said
She'd send my supper here. I've been out-
doors
All day at Ardsley—golf—played well
to-day.
And by the way, we asked a girl out there
—A decent girl, you know—to join a four-
some;
And what do you suppose she said, not
meaning it
At all, referring as she thought to one
Of the sticks? 'I never play,' she said, 'don't
know
A thing about it, shouldn't even know
Which end of the caddy to use.'

[*They all laugh*]

Good, isn't it!
Wonderful figure when she tried a stroke,

And a lovely face, no paint, fresh lips,
  young, young!
You ought to have that kind of girl.   I'm
  tired
Of all your girls!   I come here still because
I like you, Tiger.
  [*Looking round*]
                    I'm tired of Annabel.

ANNABEL.
  [*With a deep bow*]
  Oh, thank you, Willie.

WILLIE.
                    —Cassie, all of them,
  The same old faces.   Haven't you something
    new?

TIGER.
  I'm tired, Willie, of that same old question.
  [*A sudden sobbing is heard in the inner
  bedroom*]

WILLIE.
  Listen!
    [*It dies away into a moan*]
    What was that, Tiger?

TIGER.

> [*Crossing and whispering in his ear with a smile*]

'Something new!'

WILLIE.

What do you mean? A new one? In that
room?

TIGER.

Come here now, dearie!—On your honor,
sir,
As a friend and gentleman—repeat it,
please!

WILLIE.

Well, Tiger, on my honor——

TIGER.

If I put
You wise to a professional master-stroke,
You will not preach nor peach?

WILLIE.

I swear.

TIGER.

Willie,
The 'something new' was brought here——

WILLIE.

                        Never mind
    The story; is she young?

TIGER.

                        Young as they come,
    And new to it,—in fact rebellious, dear,
    And fasting for her pains.

WILLIE.

                        I'll break her in!

TIGER.
    The Baron's a much better hand at it.

WILLIE.
    Oh, come! It's an adventure!—let me try!
    She'll trust me, Tige, I look so fatherly.

TIGER.
    No, no,—some other time.   There's nothing
        in it.

WILLIE.
    But, darling, an experience and different!
    Girls like me, Tiger. Come on, let me try!
    I'll make it worth your while.

TIGER.

                              Well, you may have
Your supper with her, if you want to pay
Big money.

WILLIE.

                    Sure.   I'm rich to-night.   I won
A case last week.   And I am going to win
Another case to-night,—you know, a case
Of love at first sight.   That's how I feel!

TIGER.

                                        Go in.
And don't believe the fiction that you'll hear.
She's peevish now, that's all.   You know
         these girls
And their romances and their grievances.
Help her forget them, Willie.
    [*She takes a key out of her pocket and
    puts it in the lock of the bedroom door,
    then turns before she opens the door*]
                              Pommery?
WILLIE.
    [*Nodding*]
And a tasty little supper for your Willie!

TIGER.

   [Unlocking the door]
Remember now, you're not to preach——

WILLIE.

                       Nor peach.

TIGER.

   Promise!

WILLIE.

   I promise. Wish me good luck, Tiger!
*[She opens the door for him; he enters
the bedroom. There is a pause, then, inside the bedroom, a scream of mingled
terror and joy from the girl, and a moan
from the man]*

MARGARET.

   [Her voice is heard, heartrending]
Father! Father, I knew you'd come!
   Father!

WILLIE.

   *[Reappearing and facing the women,
livid]*
Give me her clothes! Damn you, give me
   her clothes!

[*Tiger stands motionless, petrified. Annabel crosses as in a nightmare and picks up Margaret's clothes from the couch. As she pulls them across the table, the poker-chips are dragged to the floor. Annabel turns at the sound and looks down at the poker-chips, dazed. Willie re-enters the bedroom. Annabel suddenly drops the clothes on the floor and runs out into the hall. Tiger stands motionless*]

CURTAIN

CYCLE

To Kahlil Gibran

[*The scene is a thickly furnished library in the home of a Prussian officer. Books are all about in ornate cases. There is a double door at the back, a fire-place at the left and, over a book-case at the right, a long narrow stained-glass window designed about a coat-of-arms. Friedrich the officer, leaning over a desk at the left, is indicating to his wife, Rosa, certain points in a map of Asia Minor*]

ELISABETH.

[*A girl of fifteen, entering*]

Please, father, may I show my friends the
    snap-shots?—

The ones you took?

FRIEDRICH.

[*Handing them to her from a desk-drawer*]

               Yes, Elsa, certainly.

[*She runs happily out with the photographs*]

ROSA.

Why did you laugh at what I asked you,
Friedrich?
Because it was untrue?—ridiculous?

FRIEDRICH.

Why do you listen to a servant, Rosa?

ROSA.

It was untrue?

FRIEDRICH.

Where is the girl?

ROSA.

She's gone.

FRIEDRICH.

So, after listening to a servant's gossip,
You've joined the enemy, have you?

ROSA.

Friedrich, no!

FRIEDRICH.

When I come home from war, home to my
wife,
You accuse me—

ROSA.

No.   I only asked.

FRIEDRICH.

Don't ask.
Do you teach our little girl, Elisabeth,
To ask such questions?

ROSA.

No.

FRIEDRICH.

Teach her good sense.
Teach her to keep her servants in their place.
Who was this servant?   How should she
    have news
Of what went on in Syria?

ROSA.

Through her husband.

FRIEDRICH.
A soldier?

ROSA.

Yes.   An orderly.

FRIEDRICH.

The name!

ROSA.
I don't remember.

FRIEDRICH.

Your own servant's name?

ROSA.
She left so soon.

FRIEDRICH.
[*Laughing*]

She said we fattened them,
We fattened them before we tasted them,
Plump Syrian pheasants for an officer's
    table—
And my wife believed her!

ROSA.

No, I only asked.

Friedrich.

[*Reasonably*]

The Turks, of course, were on their own
behavior.

It seems that in hot countries men must
change

Their ladies, like their linen, frequently.

Perhaps, if we'd remained there long
enough,

Even the rest of us—

Rosa.

She said the Turks—

The Turkish officers—would seldom join,

But the northerners—

Friedrich.

[*Interrupting sternly*]

We do our duty, Rosa.

They wanted the world for themselves and
they had to be shown,

French, English, Russians—

Rosa.

But not Syrians!

FRIEDRICH.

Yes.

They'd be our enemies too, if they were free.
They have to be shown, as the others had to
be shown,
That the sooner we enjoy our place in the
sun,
The better for them all.   We frighten them.
It isn't pleasant work.   It's part of war.

ROSA.

This wretched war!

FRIEDRICH.

This necessary war.
God willed it.

ROSA.

Not the God I pray to.

FRIEDRICH.

Christ?
Did you decide this with your servant too?

ROSA.

Are you deciding it, Friedrich, for a servant?

FRIEDRICH.
Did she particularize?
[*Sarcastic*]
You should have asked
The name and date and place.

ROSA.
In Lebanon,
Ten months ago, she said.

FRIEDRICH.
The filthy liar!

ELISABETH.
[*Running in again, with the photographs*]
They loved the camels and the funny houses.
And look at this one.

FRIEDRICH.
[*Taking it*]
What? I didn't mean—
Was that among them?

ELISABETH.
All those little girls—
Was it a school?

FRIEDRICH.

                         Perhaps.

ELISABETH.

                              And look at her.
    How old was this girl?

FRIEDRICH.

                              I don't know.   Fifteen.

ELISABETH.
    She looks like Cousin Gretel.

ROSA.
        [*Taking it from her husband*]
                              Let me see.

ELISABETH.
    What were they doing all alone like that,
    If it's not a school.   And, father, look,
        please tell me,
    Why were their heads hung down?   What
        made them turn
    Their faces?   Look at that one!

ROSA.
        [*In a low tone*]
                         They were afraid.

FRIEDRICH.

It was the sun.   Here, let me have it, Rosa.
[*Taking it and crushing it in his hand*]
It's not worth keeping.

ELISABETH.

Father, please, I want it!
The girl like Gretel—the pretty one!

FRIEDRICH.

It's torn.

I'm sorry.

ELISABETH.

Perhaps she isn't torn.   Please look.
I want it, father!

FRIEDRICH.

Where are your manners gone?
Your mother's spoiled you while I've been
away.

ELISABETH.

I want it.

FRIEDRICH.
          Answer me, Elisabeth.
     Are you a Prussian, dear?—or something
          else?

ELISABETH.
     I'm Prussian, father.

FRIEDRICH.
                    Be a Prussian, then.
     Obedience, dear, and self-control, it's these
     On which the state depends.   And we look
          to you,
     You future citizens, to prove our faith
     And pride and justify our victory.
     How can you be a Prussian and not rule
     Yourself?

ELISABETH.
               I'm sorry, father.   I'll be good.

ROSA.
     And do we always practise what we preach?

FRIEDRICH.
     I'm going out for half an hour.

ELISABETH.

Take me?

FRIEDRICH.
Another time.

ELISABETH.
May I come to the door with you?

FRIEDRICH.
[*Throwing the crumpled photograph into the fireplace*]

Of course.
[*When they have gone, Rosa uncreases the picture and looks at it—and then away from it, her fingers closing on the fragments*]

ELISABETH.
[*Calling gaily from outside*]
Mother! O mother, quick!

ROSA.
[*Tearing the picture into smaller bits*]
What is it, dear?
[*Appearing*]

ELISABETH.
> They were sending him away! Can't he
> > come in?
> [*Whispering*]
> A funny foreigner with things to sell.

ROSA.
> We don't need anything.

ELISABETH.
> > > Mother, we might!

ROSA.
> > > > > It's war-time.

ELISABETH.
> O let him show them to us—for my birthday!
> You said you'd buy me something for my
> > birthday.
> We might find just the thing!

ROSA.
> [*Smiling, yiolding*]
> > > > Well,—if you like.

ELISABETH.
> [*Turning, while her mother throws the
> tiny fragments back into the fireplace*]

Come in. Yes, mother says you may. In here.

[*A little bearded Foreigner enters, dark and bent. His right arm is gone. Under his left he is carrying a red box, tied with rope*]

Rosa.

[*Apologetically*]

We may not buy from you.

The Foreigner.

[*In a low quaver, like that of an old priest*]

You need not buy.

Rosa.

Our money goes for war-work now, you know.

The Foreigner.

Beautiful things are what I love—not money. And if you do not take them, I still have them.

Rosa.

[*As he unties the box*]

From Turkey?

THE FOREIGNER.
[*Indicating his lost arm*]
From the war.

ROSA.

Poor man, I see.

THE FOREIGNER.
If they'd not taken my heart, I'd have it still.
[*Beating his breast dully*]
Isn't it strange, lady?—I have no heart!

ROSA.
It's taken all our hearts and broken them,
This war.

THE FOREIGNER.
They call it war.

ELISABETH.
[*As the box opens*]
O mother, see!
Beautiful things!
[*She takes some of them out carefully*]

THE FOREIGNER.

> [*In a broken half-mad wail*]
>> All of them dead!—dead!

ROSA.

Don't, please.   You frighten her.

THE FOREIGNER.

> [*Turning toward the door, with soft cunning*]
>> I've something here—
> Something to show her.
> [*While they examine his laces, he looks outside, then comes in and deftly locks the door, without their noticing*]

THE FOREIGNER.

>> Something here to show her.
> [*He lifts out all the laces in a heap and holds up to them a long dark lock of hair*]

ROSA.

> [*With an uneasy laugh*]
> O no, no!   Not for us.

THE FOREIGNER.
[*Wailing again*]

Yes! Yes! For you!
This loveliest ·thing! This thing that was
alive!
[*To Elisabeth*]
Look at it! Touch it!

ELISABETH.
[*Startled*]

No!

ROSA.

Please—not to her!
Tell me. I'm older. I will understand.
Go, Elsa, quick!

THE FOREIGNER.

Why go? Are you so young?
[*Holding up the lock of hair*]
She was as young!

ELISABETH.
[*Clinging to Rosa*]

O mother, I'm afraid!

THE FOREIGNER.

She was afraid. They tore her from her
mother,

They tore her hands away, they whipped her
hands.

They gashed her mother's forehead with a
gun.

They cut her father's arm off, stabbed him
down.

They dragged her with the rest and watched
her, watched her.

Lest she bite open a vein in her wrist and
die.

As another girl had done. They watched
her, watched her.

They fed her milk and wine and made her
eat.

And then they came and tied her arms, they
tied her.

And gave her to the man who had chosen
her . . .

Two nights he had her; then they handed her

To other men like him, then common men—

And men and men, till she was sick and done

And hideous and mad. And then they threw
her.

My daughter's murdered body, still alive,
Into a well, into a deep cold well.
"Nobody'll drink from there for a good
    long while,
Nobody'll drink from there for a good
    long while"—
That's what they said and left her, and she
    died
And, ever since, I have tried to come to you,
    [*Slowly approaching them*]
To come to you, to come and tell you this.
What do you think now of the man you love?
What do you think of him?

ROSA.

               Merciful God!

THE FOREIGNER.
I am a Syrian, come from Lebanon—
From all those Syrian homes!

ROSA.

            But not our fault!
For God's sake, don't! I'll give you any-
    thing!
    [*Elisabeth beats at the door and screams
    wildly*]

THE FOREIGNER.
    [*Shouting*]
    What do I want but this?   Nothing but this!
    [*Throwing his revolver down and seizing
    Elisabeth*]
    Then I can die.
    [*He starts back, hearing heavy blows on
    the outside of the door.   With the force
    of its breaking open, Elisabeth falls to
    the floor.   Friedrich, entering, instantly
    thrusts his sword through the foreigner.
    Pausing only a second, Rosa, who has
    picked up the foreigner's revolver, shoots
    her husband*]

ROSA.
    [*Facing her daughter in terror and pity
    and hope*]
                Elisabeth!

ELISABETH.
    [*Slowly, with wide eyes*]
                Yes, mother.

                CURTAIN

To Isadora Duncan

*You exclaimed one day, "If only there were a simple
English text of Iphigenia as human as the Greek, no
rhymes, no inversions, no loss of meaning in the sound!"
And when I wrote you this, you liked and used it.
Therefore the blame or praise be partly yours.*

On the seashore stands a great Temple, with steps leading to a blood-stained altar. Iphigenia, the Priestess, comes out of the Temple.

IPHIGENIA.
 Pelops, the son of Tantalus, by speed
 Of chariot earned a bride, who bore him Atreus.
 And Atreus had two sons, one Menelaus,
 The other Agamemnon, who in turn
 By Clytemnestra had a child, and I
 Am she, Iphigenia.
      It is thought
 That I was sacrificed by my own father
 To Artemis, in the great quest of Helen,
 Upon an altar near the bay of Aulis,
 There where the long deep waves are caught and
      broken
 Hither and thither by the winds. That bay
 Held Agamemnon's fleet, the thousand ships
 From Hellas, waiting to avenge on Troy
 The wrong done Menelaus by the loss
 Of Helen. But a storm came up and still

169

Another storm, and neither sea nor wind
Would favor Agamemnon. So he asked
Calchas the soothsayer to consult the flame.
And this is what was answered: " Agamemnon,
Captain of Hellas, there can be no way
Of setting free thy ships till Artemis
Has had fulfilled Her promised sacrifice.
For thou hadst vowed to sacrifice each year
The fairest thing the year produced. And due
To Her long since was one whom Clytemnestra
Bore thee, the fairest of the year, thy daughter
Iphigenia . . . Let her be brought and killed."
    They sent Odysseus with his lying tongue
To lure me from my mother, on the plea
That I should wed Achilles. When I came
To Aulis, they laid hold of me and led
Me to the flame, and would have struck — I saw
The knife! But Artemis deceived their eyes,
Leaving a deer instead, and stole me through
The radiant blue until She set me down
Here in the town of Tauris, where there live
Barbaric men ruled by their uncouth King,
Thoas, a rider reckless as the wind.
He made of me a priestess in Her Temple,
And here I serve Her on Her festal days.
It has a holy sound, that word, but far
From holy are the rites I . . . Yet I dare
Not question. Dumbly I must sacrifice
To Her delight strangers who happen here.

It was their custom long before I came.
My hands ordain the victim. Other hands,
Inside the Inner Temple, drain his blood,
Which then is poured upon this altar-stone.

(*She comes down the steps*)

I dreamed last night a deathly dream.   Perhaps
The morning will dispel it if I speak it.
I dreamed myself at home again in Argos,
Asleep among my maidens — when a roll
Of thunder shook the ground. I ran outside.
I watched the house. I saw the coping fall.
Then the whole palace plunged from roof to base.
Only one column stood untouched, of all
My father's home. And that one stood alive,
A man with bright brown hair and breathing lips.
Then I began unwillingly to touch
His brow with the water that means woe to
    strangers —
And with the tears of my interpretation.
    Must it not mean Orestes? — Dead, dead!
It was my brother whom I touched with tears.
The pillar of a family is the son,
And in those waters is the sign of death.
, Let me then pour the funeral-cup, for him
Who is too far away for nearer rites.

(*She goes up the steps again*)

Come now, my maidens, my Hellenic maidens,
O captives of the king! — Enslaved to serve
The living, let us freely serve the dead.
    I must go in and pray, then call to them
By the great summons of the Temple-bell.

(She goes into the Temple)

ORESTES.

(Cautiously following Pylades toward the Temple)

Take care lest someone should be coming by!

PYLADES.
I looked both ways and there is no one coming.

ORESTES.
Is this the Shrine of Artemis, which we
Set out from Argos over many seas
To find?   O Pylades! — is this the Shrine?

PYLADES.
I think it is, Orestes. So dost thou.

ORESTES.
Is that the stone, dark with the blood of Greeks?

PYLADES.
If ever I saw blood — look, on the edge!

ORESTES.

And there beneath the roof, spoils of the dead!

PYLADES.

Trophies of strangers whom these men have murdered.

ORESTES.

Be careful how thou goest then — be watchful!

Why has Thy oracle, O Phœbus, sent
This thing upon me and the sight of blood
Again? Have I not seen enough of blood?
My mother shed my father's blood, I hers.
And then the Furies, with their eyes bloody,
Hunted me down, a wanderer through the world —
Till fugitive I went to Thee, to pray
An end of all the cycles of despair
That sped me, maddened me, hurled me through
        Hellas.
Thy answer came: "Go seek the Taurian land
Where Artemis my Sister has Her Shrine.
Discover there Her effigy that fell
From Heaven into the Temple. Then by skill
Or by good-fortune take it and proceed
Surviving every hazard, and convey
The Image to the holy land of Athens."
No more was said, except that by this deed
I was to be relieved of my afflictions . . .

And here I am, O Phœbus, far from home
Upon this dismal shore — obeying Thee.

Now, Pylades, companion of my task,
What course are we to take?   To scale these walls
Would be impossible.   Are we to climb
The open stairs? — and so be seen?   Are we
To force the brazen locks, not knowing where
They lead?   For if they come upon us here,
It will be certain death.   Shall we not turn
In time and take our ship?   O, let me face
The Furies, rather than inflict this thing
On thee!

PYLADES.

    What do we know of flight?   How dare
We take a course of which our hearts know nothing?
Why should we disobey Apollo's voice
And offer Him dishonor?   No!   There must
Be ways.   Come, let us leave the Temple, hide
Ourselves in some dark cave and shun the ship
Lest it should be attacked and we be captured.
    Look! through that opening between the beams
A man might lower himself inside the wall! —
A coward drops the cup.   But a brave man's drink
Is hardship.   And by all the Gods shall we,
Coming as far as this, now at the end turn back?

ORESTES.

No.   Thou art saying what I too should say.

So let us go and find our hiding-place.
Phœbus would never tolerate defeat
Of His commandment. Come! Have we not
  youth? —
Add youth to courage, we can move the world.

(*They go out*)

(*The great bell rings. One by one the Temple
  Maidens assemble*)

A MAIDEN.
O ye who dwell upon these Clashing Rocks
  That guard the Euxine Sea,
Keep silence now before Latona's Daughter,
Artemis, Goddess of the pointed hills!

(*Turning toward the Altar*)

O Artemis, I come
On consecrated feet into Thy court,
  I hail Thee beautiful
In Thy gold dome above the colonnades!

A SECOND MAIDEN.
Thy priestess calls me, she who keeps Thy keys,
  Who left behind, for Thee,
Her land of Hellas, the embattled walls,
The shore of horses, and the quiet fields

Wherein my father lived.
I must obey her call and worship Thee
    In this embittered land
Far from Eurotas and from happiness.

A THIRD MAIDEN.

(*Going to Iphigenia, who enters from the Temple*)

O daughter of the king that gathered ships
    A thousand strong and led
Unnumbered men against high-towering Troy,
I heard thee call and I have come to thee.
    Why hast thou summoned us?
What makes thy cheek so thoughtful and so pale?
    What has thy tongue to tell,
That thy brow is dark and bowed upon thy hands?

IPHIGENIA.
My maidens, listen! Listen while I tell
What I have seen. The Muse has hid Her face
And I am mourning for a kinsman lost.
Last night I had a dream of destiny.
O weep with me!—I saw my brother dead!
My dream was clear. My father's house is ended,
My race broken and gone, Orestes dead!
    What anguish, Argos, art thou made to bear
When Fate pursues me still and takes from me
My only brother!—

To the vanished dead
Let me now pour this offering, this gift
Upon the earth, commingled of the milk
Of mountain-kine and of the wine of Bacchus
And of the honey that the russet bees
Gathered,— a soothing gift for him I loved.
Give me the heavy urn of gold, to hold
My offering to the God of Death.
This urn,
Orestes, son of Agamemnon, thou
That liest dead beneath the earth, I bring
And pour for thee. Better I cannot bring,
I cannot bring to thee my heavy locks,
I cannot lay them, weeping, on thy grave.
And yet, though men believe me long since dead,
I still can weep, far from my home and thee.

A FOURTH MAIDEN.
O Lady, woe is in me for thy woe,
My song is like the song
Of old that mourners in the far-off east
Chant for the dead, reciting only death,
The very song of hell,
A wail of no returning and no hope,
Using no note of glory,
Only the desolation of the grave.

THE FIRST MAIDEN.
Mourn for the sons of Atreus, in whose house

The hearth can never burn!
Mourn for their bitter heritage, a home
That waits the coming of some happy King
    But cannot give him welcome!
Trouble is born forever in their sky
    Since Phœbus turned His car
Of toppling horses out of the course of joy.

THE THIRD MAIDEN.

There was desired long since a golden lamb,
    And out of the dispute
Mischief arose to tantalize thy house . . .

THE FOURTH MAIDEN.

Vengeance has made its unappeasèd way
    With every dart of death
And visited thy family one by one,
    And now with eager hand
Fate is pursuing thee. Thy turn has come.

IPHIGENIA.

O bitter my beginning in the womb
Of her who bore me, from the very night
That she conceived! Appointed by the Fates
To suffer in this world, I was a child
Accursed. Yet how she cherished me, her first-born,
And thrilled that I, of all the girls of Argos,
Should be a bride upon the way to Troy!
    What had she borne me for and loved me for? —

To come to nothing, through my father's fault!
To come, behind the horses of delight,
Not to Achilles — but to grief and horror!
    And now beside this melancholy sea
I live my days — lonely, no love, no friends,
Wife of no man and mother of no child.
I know no home. I sing no Argive song
With Argive women to the Queen of Heaven.
I weave upon the whirring loom no tale
Of Pallas routing Titans . . . O, instead,
I see an altar stained with bloody death.
I hear the cry for pity and the moans
Of men — a woe too hideous to be told.
    Yet even that is little to me now —
Now that a throne is empty and his eyes
Are past all weeping, as I wish mine were.
For I who loved Orestes all those years
Shall never see him now but as I left him,
A little baby at his mother's breast —
I who had thought to see him as a King.

THE SECOND MAIDEN.
    Look! — from the beach a herdsman comes to thee,
    Comes like a man with news!

HERDSMAN.

    (*Arriving breathless*)

  O daughter of the house of Agamemnon,

I have a thing to tell!

IPHIGENIA.
    Is it a thing
To warrant this intrusion?

HERDSMAN.
    Yes . . . A ship
From sea has rounded the Symplegades
And in the mist two men have come ashore,
Young, worthy to be offered on the altar!
Make ready then the Feast of Artemis!

IPHIGENIA.
Where are they from? — what country? Couldst
    thou tell?

HERDSMAN.
From Hellas, but I could not say what part.

IPHIGENIA.
What were their names? Thou must have heard
    their names!

HERDSMAN.
One of them called the other " Pylades."

IPHIGENIA.
And the one who spoke?

HERDSMAN.
   We did not hear his name.

IPHIGENIA.
   Where were they captured?

HERDSMAN.
   Down beside the sea.

IPHIGENIA.
   What were you herdsmen doing by the sea?

HERDSMAN.
   Washing our cattle there.

IPHIGENIA.
   But answer me,
   How were they captured?   It is new to me
   And unbelievable.   For all this time
   Has passed and never brought a Greek before
   To bleed in sacrifice — never a Greek.

HERDSMAN.
   Just as we drove our cattle from the woods
   In that long hollow where the curling tide
   Has cut away the cliff, where fishers rest
   From purple-fishing, one of us ahead
   Came stealing back on tiptoe and he warned us:
   " They are not men but Gods!   Behind that rock! —

Not men but Gods!" And then another herds-
    man,
Caught sight of them, raised up his hands and
    prayed:
"God in whose keeping are all ships, Palæmon! —
Have mercy on us, whether these be Sons
Of Zeus or Brothers of the Fifty Nereids!"
But another mocked our fear and laughed aloud,
Daring the possible anger of the Gods.
For he maintained there must have been a wreck
And these were mariners who chose that cave
To hide in, having heard that strangers here
Are sacrificed. And he persuaded most
Of us; and we were planning what to do
To capture them — when one of them came out
Into full view and, standing there a moment,
Stared not at us nor anything we saw
But straight above him, groaning, shuddering,
And bent his head from one side to the other
Behind his arms, like one delirious,
And then cried out as sharply as a hunter:
"Look, Pylades! O look at her! O look!
There! — there! Dost thou not see her now? —
    that Fury
From hell! Look at the serpent on her head
With mouth wide open, writhing for my blood
Another! — and another! Look at her
High on the cliff, belching a flame at me
And holding in her hands my mother's body

Till she can hurl it down on me and kill me!
O they are all around me! Pylades!"
And we could tell by the motion of his head
When the dogs barked or when the cattle lowed
That some invisible Fury mocking him
Became to him in every sound a threat.

In our amazement we were sitting there
Like stricken men — when out he whipped his sword
And, quick as a lion, leapt upon our herd
As if attacking Furies there. He slashed
Their sides with might and main until the rim
Of the sea was rolling thick with gore. We saw
Our herd wounded and dying and we looked
For sticks to arm ourselves and blew our horns
For help. And then when slowly we approached
      him —
His madness left him. I can see him now
Standing a moment. While I watch he drops
In a heap and foaming at the lips. Our chance! —
Our chance! Forward we hurried with our
      cudgels
And rocks. But still his comrade, unafraid,
Leaned over him and wiped his lips and held
A linen fold above his face protecting him —
Till suddenly the fallen man stood up
Calm and himself again and saw the rush
Of stones that neared him like a breaking wave.
He gave one groan as we surrounded him;
And then we heard his voice ring clear and say:

"Death, Pylades! Then let us meet it well —
Like men! Out with thy sword and follow me!"
　　Back from the glittering swords we ran, to lure
Them to the glen. For there when some of us
Would run to shelter others could hurl rocks
To draw the pursuers off and then could fly
And let the first come back again with stones.
And yet the destined offering stood clean.
For, strange as it may sound, of all the stones
We volleyed at those men, not one went true!
All we could hope for was to wear them out.
So, working round them in a ring, we struck
Their swords with stones, until they lost their hold
And had no breath for the recovery.
　　And then we took them captive to the King,
Who ordered us to bring them here to thee
To be prepared and bled for Artemis.

Ask Artemis, O priestess, to direct
Other such wanderers as these to Tauris!
Let men from Hellas shed their blood for thine
Which men from Hellas clamored for at Aulis!

The First Maiden.
　　This is no common man who came away
　　From the land of Hellas to an alien shore
　　　　And battled like a God!

Iphigenia.
　　Go back and bring me the two mariners.

I shall be ready for them with the rites.

(*Exit the Herdsman*)

Poor heart of mine, which in the days gone by
Was tender and compassionate to strangers,
And even yesterday grew pitiful
At thought of men from Hellas coming here,
A cruel dream has changed thee overnight.
For since Orestes is no more alive,
Now, where my heart was, there is only
    stone
And you who come today, no matter who,
Will find in me a woman without tears.

Friends, by my own unhappiness I know
That the experience of evil days
Brings disregard for lesser sufferers.
   No heaven-sent wind has ever forced a ship
Between the Clashing Rocks, bringing me Helen,
That Helen whom I hate, and Menelaus,
That I might make of them the sacrifice,
Let a new Aulis expiate the old —
And have my vengeance! — It was Helen's fault
And his, that Greek hands lifted me at Aulis
And led me like a beast before the altar —
Where he who held the knife was my own father.
   I live it all again. My hands groping
Go out to him again and touch his beard

And cling about his knees. I cry to him:
" O thou thyself, thyself, hast brought me here!
Thou hast deceived my maidens and my mother!
They sing my marriage-song at home, they fill
The house with happiness . . . and all the
     time
Here am I dying — slain, father, by thee!
Thou hast led me in thy chariot, to take
Achilles for my lord. But here is death —
And on my lips no kiss but only blood!"
     And I had left my home with my white veil
Drawn down. I had not taken in my arms
My brother, who is dead, nor kissed my sister.
I had saved all my kisses and embraces
For him I thought to marry . . . Yet my heart
Was homesick even then and ached with hope
That I should soon come back again to Argos.

And thou art dead, Orestes, and thou too
Foregoest our inheritance, our home!

O what has Artemis desired of me? —
She who forbids Her court to any man
Whose hand is stained with bloodshed or with touch
Of childbirth or of burial, calls him
Unclean and bans him — She so scrupulous
In all these things — will yet receive the blood
Of human beings on Her altar-stone?
It is not credible. Latona bore
To Zeus no daughter so unkind! The thing

Is no more true than are the tales they tell
Of Tantalus preparing for the Gods
A child whom They devoured . . . Artemis,
These people being murderers themselves,
Impute to Thee their own iniquity.—
No!—I will not believe it of a God!

THE SECOND MAIDEN.

Who can these be that left the holy streams
    Of Dirce, or the reeds
Green-growing in Eurotas, to prefer
This bitter beach, to dare the ominous rocks
    Where the seas meet in fog,
Where Artemis, among Her colonnades
    Demanding sacrifice,
Receives upon Her altars human blood?

THE FOURTH MAIDEN.

Why have they urged the oarsmen on their ship
    To shake the clinging sea
With a great stroke, and to accelerate
With rush of rivalry the racing wind?
    Was it to sweep the shores
For riches and to vie in bearing home,
    Each to upbuild his house,
The treasures and the trophies of the world?

That glittering hope is immemorial
    And beckons many men

To their undoing. Ever insatiate,
They sail the sea and look to foreign towns
    To fill their ships with spoil.
But some men never find prosperity,
    For all their voyaging;
While others find it with no voyaging.

THE THIRD MAIDEN.

How have they passed the peril of the rocks
    That clash? and of the beach
Of Phineus heavy with broken waves?
How have they turned their rudder to the land
    Where the Fifty Nereids
Hand in hand dance and circle round and sing,
    Where the wings of ocean brood,
And where Achilles rode by the dark water?

THE FIRST MAIDEN.

My Lady prayed that Fate might hither bring,
    On the way home from Troy,
The cause of her great misery. O would
That Helen, Helen had been blown ashore,
    That on her fatal head,
For recompense, the holy drops might fall
    And that my Lady's knife
Might find in her the fitting sacrifice!

THE SECOND MAIDEN.

But I have prayed for a deliverer,

Some mariner from Hellas
Able to end our pain and set us free.
Ever I go, though only in a dream,
    Back to my father's home . . .
No man has greater riches than the joy
    That comes to us in visions —
They cannot take away from us our dreams.

THE THIRD MAIDEN.
    Look where they come! — two captives bound in
        chains!
        The herdsman's news was true!
    Hush for the offering to Artemis!

THE SECOND MAIDEN.
    See, Hellas, how thy hands are impotent·
        To change this ritual!

THE FOURTH MAIDEN.
    O Artemis, if Tauris in Thy sight
        Win favor by this gift,
    Assert Thy custom and receive this blood!

IPHIGENIA.
    Let me now think of none but Artemis
    And serve Her with the worship She demands.

    Loosen their hands.   For in this holy court
    Chains are unhallowed things. Enter the Temple.

Prepare the altar for the ritual.

(Turning to the captives)

I wonder who your mother was? — your father? —
Whether you had a sister who has lost
Her brothers and laments their bravery? —
Invisible and mute, Fate comes and goes
And never whispers where Her blow shall fall;
None of us ever sees Her in the dark
Or understands Her cruel mysteries.
Tell me, unhappy men, where are you from? —
You who are far from home and yet must go
Farther away from home even than this!

ORESTES.
What woman art thou, weeping for our lot?
What can we mean to thee, to draw thy pity,
To make our tribulation difficult?
    There is no wisdom in lamenting death
And only fools, when they behold it near,
Meet it with tears. The man who doubles death
By the cowardice of pitying himself
Earns for himself contempt as well as death . . .
Let us accept our fortune as it comes —
No pity and no tears! We dared our fate.
And what we undertook — we undertook.

IPHIGENIA.
One of your names was brought me by a herdsman.

Tell me then, which of you is Pylades?

ORESTES.
He, if it does thee any good to know.

IPHIGENIA.
And from what town in Hellas?

ORESTES.
Does it matter?

IPHIGENIA.
And are you brothers?

ORESTES.
In all else but birth.

IPHIGENIA.
And what may I call thee?

ORESTES.
Unfortunate!

IPHIGENIA.
That would be pity's name for thee, not mine.

ORESTES.
Then say I have no name and call me nothing.

IPHIGENIA.
Art thou so jealous for thy reputation?

ORESTES.
Come, sacrifice my body, not my name!

IPHIGENIA.
Thou wilt not even name for me thy town?

ORESTES.
I am so soon a townsman of no town.

IPHIGENIA.
Surely it is not much to tell me that.

ORESTES.
Ah, but it is — when one can answer, " Argos "!

IPHIGENIA.
Argos? not Argos? thou art not from Argos?

ORESTES.
My town, Mycenæ, was a lordly place.

IPHIGENIA.
Then what could bring thee from it? — banish-
    ment?

ORESTES.
A kind of banishment — yet self-imposed.

IPHIGENIA.
  How fortunate to see a son of Argos!

ORESTES.
  But not to be one in thy company!

IPHIGENIA.
  And let me ask about another town —

ORESTES.
  But why this questioning?

IPHIGENIA.
    O tell me news
  Of that most talked-of town in all the world!
  What hast thou heard of Troy?

ORESTES.
    By all the Gods,
  I wish that I had never heard its name!

IPHIGENIA.
  But is it true that Troy is overthrown?

ORESTES.
  Its towers lie broken in the dust.

IPHIGENIA.
    And Helen?
  Has Menelaus taken Helen back?

ORESTES.
And soon repented. For she brings him sorrow.

IPHIGENIA.
She brought me sorrow too. Where is she now?

ORESTES.
Gone back with him to Sparta.

IPHIGENIA.
How I hate
The name of Helen! How all Hellas hates it!

ORESTES.
I have my own good cause for hating it.

IPHIGENIA.
Did the Achæans return home contented?

ORESTES.
It would take many tongues to answer that.

IPHIGENIA.
But tell me quickly, while there still is time!

ORESTES.
Then ask me quickly. I will answer thee.

IPHIGENIA.
What of the soothsayer, Calchas? Where is he?

ORESTES.
　Reported dead at home.

IPHIGENIA.
　　O Artemis,
　Hail for that news!　And is Odysseus dead?

ORESTES.
　Neither at home nor dead — but wandering.

IPHIGENIA.
　O how I pray he never reach his home!

ORESTES.
　Why wish him that?　Has he not borne enough?

IPHIGENIA.
　What of Achilles?

ORESTES.
　　Dead.　His marriage planned
　At Aulis never happened.

IPHIGENIA.
　　Those who knew
　About that plan knew it a cruel lie.

ORESTES.
　Knowing these things, art thou thyself from Hellas?

IPHIGENIA.
  I was, but lost my home long, long ago.

ORESTES.
  No wonder thou art asking me these questions!

IPHIGENIA.
  What of that king they called The Happy King?

ORESTES.
  The one I think thou meanest was not happy.

IPHIGENIA.
  I ask of Agamemnon.

ORESTES.
    I know nothing,
  Nothing of him.   O ask me no more questions!

IPHIGENIA.
  But no news must be good news!   Say it is!

ORESTES.
  The news is death — his and another's death.

IPHIGENIA.
  O Agamemnon!   O King Agamemnon!

ORESTES.
  Could he be kin to thee, thou carest so?

IPHIGENIA.
Remembering his glory and his pride!

ORESTES.
All of it ended by his own wife's hand.

IPHIGENIA.
O! — Pitiable woman! Poor, poor king!

ORESTES.
Ask me no more, I beg, not one word more!

IPHIGENIA.
But is she living? Answer me but that!

ORESTES.
Her own son killed her.

IPHIGENIA.
Why?

ORESTES.
To be avenged
On her who killed his father.

IPHIGENIA.
How exact
He was, how just! Yet how I pity him!

ORESTES.
  And well thou mayest. No God pities him.

IPHIGENIA.
  Not one of Agamemnon's children left?

ORESTES.
  Electra, yes. But loses him she loves!

IPHIGENIA.
  What has been said of her they sacrificed?

ORESTES.
  Nothing of her, except that she is dead.

IPHIGENIA.
  O miserable king, willing to slay her!

ORESTES.
  O wicked war caused by a wicked woman,
  And all the waste and wicked consequence!

IPHIGENIA.
  The son of the dead king — alive in Argos?

ORESTES.
  Living, but not in Argos, not in Argos!

IPHIGENIA.
  My dream was nothing then, it lied to me!

ORESTES.
  Dreams, lies, lies, dreams,— nothing but emptiness!
  Even the Gods with all Their name for wisdom
  Have only dreams and lies and lose Their course,
  Blinded, confused and ignorant as we.
    The wisest man is he who goes his way
  And listens to no prophet guiding him.
  The fool is he who follows oracles,
  Forsaking his own judgment. Those who know
  Know such a man can only come to wreck.

THE SECOND MAIDEN.
  O who will bring us news whether our kin
    Are living or are dead!

IPHIGENIA.
  Let me suggest a plan that I have thought of,
  To our advantage, yours as well as mine.
  And nothing makes more surely for achievement
  Than interests in common. Tell me this . . .
  Wilt thou go back, if I can grant thee leave,
  Bearing for me to Argos and my friends
  A letter that has been prepared for them?
  My words were written down by one who died
  Here at my ritual but pitied me,
  Blaming his blood on Artemis, not me.
  No one had come from Hellas, not one Greek,
  Whose life might be conceded to bear home
  My message. But in thee I find a man
  Worthy to carry it, knowing the names

And places dear to me.   And so I ask
Thy help and offer in exchange thy life —
With one condition: that thy friend remain,
To pay the sacrifice to Artemis.

ORESTES.

I thank thee, Lady, for a fair proposal,
Save in that one respect.   What would my life
Be worth to me, earned by deserting him?
I am the captain of this misadventure,
And he but sailed with me to comfort me.
It would be wrong if he should pay the cost
And I repudiate my enterprise.
Thy errand shall be done — but not by me.
Give him thy confidence, give him thy letter.
To thee it makes no difference which of us
Carries the message homeward.   And to me
It makes no difference when I die or how.
But if I brought disaster on a friend
And yet myself went free, then there would be
No faith left in me, no respect, no love.
Besides, his life is dear to me as mine.
His life is mine.   For in his life — I live.

IPHIGENIA.

Thou hast a heart of gold and must be sprung
From some great seed, to be so true a friend.   .   .   .
If only the survivor of my race
May be like thee!   I have a brother left,

Although I should not know him by his face.
As thou hast chosen then, so let it be.
Thy friend shall take the letter — and thou prove
Thy love by laying down thy life for him.

ORESTES.
Whose is the hand that sacrifices me?

IPHIGENIA.
Whose hand but mine! Artemis willed it so.

ORESTES.
Thy hand! Thy poor, unenviable hand!

IPHIGENIA.
What is imposed on me I must obey.

ORESTES.
A woman hold the knife to shed men's blood!

IPHIGENIA.
Not that! — O not the knife! — Only the water,
The sacrificial water for thy brow.

ORESTES.
Who is it then that strikes the final blow?

IPHIGENIA.
Inside the Shrine are men who do that part.

ORESTES.

When I am burnt, what happens to my body?

IPHIGENIA.

They seal the ashes in a rocky cleft.

ORESTES.

O that my sister's hand might tend my body!

IPHIGENIA.

She is too far away from thee to hear
Petition for the gift she cannot give. . . .
Being from Argos, let me care for thee,
Let me do everything that she might do!
I will array thy body in rich robes —
Then pour upon the embers yellow oil
Cooling and clean and the golden essences
That bees collect from every mountain-flower,
To make thee pure and sweet. . . .
　　Now I must go
And bring my letter. I have kept it here
So long a while.— O think of me with pity.

See that you guard these men, but do not bind them.

O if at last my letter should arrive
In Argos and be opened by the hand
Of him I love, a letter never dreamed-of,
Then he would listen through the opening grave
And hear my living lips cry out to him!

(She goes into the Temple)

THE FIRST MAIDEN.
   I pity thee upon whose fated head
      The water shall be sprinkled!

ORESTES.
   But choose not pity.   Change it into hope.

THE SECOND MAIDEN.
   Let me then hope, but not for thee, for him,
      That he may come again
   Into his father's country and be blest.

PYLADES.
   But how can he be blest who leaves his friend?

THE FIRST MAIDEN.
   Or I hold back my pity for thy death?

THE FOURTH MAIDEN.
   And yet I pity thee, having to live.

THE THIRD MAIDEN.
      Which is unhappier?

THE FOURTH MAIDEN.
   I cannot tell,— I watch and cannot tell
   Whether to pity thee, or thee, the more.

ORESTES.

O Pylades, what art thou thinking of?

PYLADES.

What dost thou think that I am thinking of?

ORESTES.

This woman! Thou rememberest her questions,
Each one so apt; of the defeat of Troy,
Of the Achæans' homecoming, of Calchas,
Of Achilles, and her great concern
At Agamemnon's death and then her questions
About his wife and children? I believe
That she herself, she too, belongs in Argos! —
Or she would never send a letter there
And make all these inquiries anxiously
As if the fate of Argos were her own.

PYLADES.

Thou hast expressed what I was wondering.
And yet I thought it natural enough
That in a city at all civilized
People should ask about the fate of kings . . .
But that was not what troubled me, so much as —

ORESTES.

As what? Tell me and let me help thee solve it.

PYLADES.

How canst thou wrong me, thinking I would live

And let thee die? As I set out with thee
So shall I journey with thee to the end,
Or I should never show my face again
Among the hills of Argos, but to be
Despised and pointed out in every valley
As one who had betrayed a friend. And worse
Than that would be declared of me, the worst
That evil minds can conjure and enjoy —
Even that I had wished thy death, or caused it,
That I might profit by inheritance
And, being thy sister's husband, win thy throne.

   See how afraid I am and how ashamed
Of the very thought of leaving thee. One way,
And only one is open. Where thou goest,
Though to the knife and to the flame, I fol-
   low —
That I may be beyond a doubt thy friend.

ORESTES.

  Thou canst not be my friend and yet deny me.
I bear a load that cannot be laid down,
And wilt thou lighten thine by doubling mine?
All the humiliating shame that thou
But fearest from men's tongues would fall to me
In my own heart from my own conduct, if I let
The services thou didst me bring thee harm.

   What has Fate left me of my life to cherish
But a good ending? As for thee, my friend,
Thou hast not any right to choose to die.

Thou hast the blessing of thy happy blood
To make thee wish to live. And so I pray
That by thy life a comfort may be brought
To my afflicted house. O Pylades,
When thou art home, there with thy wife, my sister,
Beget for me, dear friend, my happiness.
Let my name live again and in thy children
The house of Agamemnon be renewed.
Therefore go back and make my home thy home.
And having come to Hellas and the shore
Where the Argive horsemen ride — give me thy
    hand
And swear that thou wilt make a grave for me
And lay on it memorials and let
My sister bring, remembering me, a lock
Of her long hair. Tell her that I was led
Before the altar by the hand of one
Who came from Argos, by a woman's hand,
And how my blood at last was purified.
O Pylades, be good to her, be true!
And fare thee well, my best and truest friend,
Loved in my boyhood when I shared my sport
Over the hills with thee and in my manhood
When my sorrows came and thou wert with me still!

By falsely prophesying, Phœbus lied
To me and tricked me; luring me away
From home, lest watchful eyes in Hellas see
That Gods, like men, can break Their promises.

I gave Him everything, my faith, my will,
I killed my mother for He bade me strike · · ·
And in return He has forsaken me.

PYLADES.
Let me obey then not myself but thee —
And build thy tomb in Hellas. Be assured
That I shall love thy sister well and always.
And having loved thee living, I shall know
How to receive thee closer in thy death · · ·
If death it be. We marvel at the Gods
And their mysterious way of keeping hid
The face of life behind a mask of death,
Then showing the true face.

ORESTES.
The time is gone
For the Gods to show that face — for she has come.

IPHIGENIA.

(Returning and addressing the Attendants)

Precede me into the Temple and be ready.

(The Attendants enter the Temple)

Here is my letter, all this length of it · · ·
Yet I have wondered. When a man arrives

Out of his danger, he forgets his fear
And sometimes he forgets his promises.
Wherefore my apprehension lest thy friend,
When he is freed and on his way again,
Forget how much this letter means to me.

ORESTES.
And what dost thou propose, to ease thy mind?

IPHIGENIA.
That he shall swear to take this where I say.

ORESTES.
And wilt thou make an oath matching his oath?

IPHIGENIA.
To do what, or undo what?

ORESTES.
    To obtain
Safe quittance for him from this wretched place.

IPHIGENIA.
What would his oath be good for, lacking mine?

ORESTES.
But will the King of Tauris let him sail?

IPHIGENIA.
I can persuade the King and will myself
Go to the ship and put thy friend aboard.

ORESTES.
Then state the oath that thou wilt have him swear.

IPHIGENIA.
Promise to give this letter to my friend.

PYLADES.
I swear to give this letter to thy friend.

IPHIGENIA.
And I to give thee safeguard from this place.

PYLADES.
Thou swearest by what name?

IPHIGENIA.
By Artemis,
Whose favor be upon me in Her temple!

PYLADES.
And I by Zeus Himself, by Heaven's King.

IPHIGENIA.
And if thou failest to fulfill thy oath?

PYLADES.
Then may I never see Argos again! —
And if thou failest in fulfilling thine?

IPHIGENIA.

Then let me fail ever to come to Argos.

PYLADES.

There is one chance that we have not considered.

IPHIGENIA.

A chance, thou meanest, that affects thy word?

PYLADES.

The oath would not be fair if it should happen
That in a storm the vessel should be wrecked
Or strike a rock and everything go down
And yet my life be saved — and not the letter.
In that event I ask to be exempted.

IPHIGENIA.

In any plan, two ways make one way sure . . .
Then let me tell thee carefully word by word
The contents of my letter, thou in turn
To tell it to my friend. And that insures us.
For either thou shalt place it in his hand
And let the silent writing speak or else
The writing, lost, shall echo still in thee.

PYLADES.

That will be safer both for thee and me.
So tell me whom to find for thee in Argos
And what to say to him.

IPHIGENIA.

Say this to him,
Say to Orestes, son of Agamemnon,
A greeting comes from one he thought was dead.
Tell him his sister is not dead at Aulis
But is alive.

ORESTES.

Alive? Iphigenia?
O no! — Unless the dead come back again!

IPHIGENIA.

Thou art beholding her, for I am she.
But let me finish what I ask of him:
" O brother, rescue me! Let me not live
The priestess of a loathly ritual! —
Let me not die forlorn, in a wild land! "

ORESTES.

Where am I, Pylades? What am I hearing?

IPHIGENIA.

" Lest thou, remembering me, shalt have no
     peace! " —
The name, thou must repeat it, is Orestes.

PYLADES.

Ye Gods!

IPHIGENIA.

Not Gods but a woman speaks to thee.

PYLADES.

It seemed I heard the Gods — and yet heard thee!
O let me listen further and make sure!

IPHIGENIA.

Tell him that Artemis put out Her hand
And spared my life at Aulis, leaving a deer
To bleed for me instead, and that my father,
Not looking when he struck, thought he slew me.
Artemis brought me here. . . . The letter ends.

PYLADES.

O what an easy oath it is to keep!
Lady, keep thine or not — I keep mine now.
I bring thee this, Orestes, from thy sister.

ORESTES.

How can I look at letters? — Come to me!
O let me look at thee whom I had lost! —
O let me touch thee with my hands and prove
That thou art real and hold thee close, close!

THE THIRD MAIDEN.

Lay not thy hands, no matter who thou art,
    Upon those holy robes! —
Bring not indignity to Artemis!

ORESTES.

Thou art my sister, my own father's daughter,
And nature will not let thee turn away
From thy own brother given back to thee.

IPHIGENIA.

Ah, thou wouldst make me think that thou art he! —
Orestes is in Argos and not here.

ORESTES.

No, my poor sister, not in Argos! — here!

IPHIGENIA.

Then was Tyndareus thy mother's father?

ORESTES.

Yes, and my father's grandfather was Pelops.

IPHIGENIA.

What art thou saying? How can I believe thee?

ORESTES.

By asking me about our father's home.

IPHIGENIA.

Then speak of it! — for I am listening! — speak!

ORESTES.

Electra used to tell us tales of Atreus
And of Thyestes, how they came to quarrel.

IPHIGENIA.

It was about a golden lamb they quarreled!

ORESTES.

And thy hands made, with fine embroideries,
A pattern of the quarrel.

IPHIGENIA.

Art thou he?
Art thou in truth my brother? — art thou he?

ORESTES.

There was a picture, on thy loom, of Phœbus
Changing His course. Hast thou forgotten that?

IPHIGENIA.

O not one thread of it have I forgotten!

ORESTES.

There was a bath of bridal fragrances
Thy mother sent to Aulis.— Thou rememberest?

IPHIGENIA.

Everything on that day I can remember —
But happiness.

ORESTES.

A lock of hair that came,
Sent to thy mother.

IPHIGENIA.

A memorial
I meant it for, commemorating me —
To mark a grave where I could never lie.

ORESTES.

And I recall a keepsake in thy room,
The ancient spear that Pelops once had used
To win his bride.

IPHIGENIA.

Orestes, O my brother!
My home has come to me from far away!
For thou art come, I have thee in my arms!

ORESTES.

And I have thee in mine, whom I thought dead!
No wonder that the tears are in our eyes! —
Of joy, not sorrow! — yet of sorrow too!

IPHIGENIA.

Thou wert a baby, when I came away,
Lifted to see me. And thy little arms
Held out to me are come to me again,
Grown strong to comfort me. How can I speak
My joy! There is no language sweet enough!
There is no joy like this. There never was!

THE FOURTH MAIDEN.

And would that we might say it need not end!

IPHIGENIA.

I am bewildered. And I cannot think
What I should say, my friends? — I cannot think
Of anything but joy — except a fear
That he might vanish as he came. O Argos,
Land of my love, my heart is full of thee,
And of my brother thou hast borne and bred
To be a living glory to thy name!

ORESTES.

We who were born to happiness have lived
And learned unhappiness.

IPHIGENIA.

    Unhappiness? —
O how I learned it when against my throat
My own unhappy father held the knife!

ORESTES.

I have a vision of his stricken face.

IPHIGENIA.

And the false marriage, when the marriage-hymn
Was made of tears! Not to Achilles' arms
I went, but to the coldness of the altar —
And felt the bitter waters on my head.

ORESTES.

Unhappy daughter and unhappy father!

IPHIGENIA.

But why have pity on a pitiless man
Who brought me all this grief?

ORESTES.

And might have brought
On thee to-day — the slaying of thy brother!

IPHIGENIA.

Some God prevented. But I came so near,
My hand was so impending on the deed,
That I am shaken with the thought of thee —
Dead! . . .
        We have seen today a miracle
Begin. How shall it end for thee and me?
How shall I speed thee safely from this place
Of horror home again? For there are swords
To face: a question fitter for thy wit
To weigh than mine, though thou art shaken too.
Shouldst thou be safer travelling by foot
Than by the ship? No, no! — I see thee go
Losing thy way among barbarians
Ashore, encompassed by a thousand deaths.
The ship is better — even that sharp return
Between the Clashing Rocks. Go! — dare the sea,
Take to the ship again! And yet who knows
If God or man shall guide thee on the sea
To liberation? — or if any chance
Can save thee now to make our home a glory?

THE THIRD MAIDEN.

I have heard marvellous tales from story-tellers,
But nothing to compare
With this event which my own eyes have seen.

PYLADES.

Orestes, it is natural for thee
To greet thy sister and recount with her
The happenings of thy house. But there are things
Of urgency to think of: our escape
Out of this land and how to compass it.
For he is wise who makes a friend of Fortune
And goes to meet her when she comes to him.

ORESTES.

Well said!— and let her be well met to-day!—
For every God helps him who helps himself.

IPHIGENIA.

But he shall tell me first about my sister,
About Electra!— Tell me of my sister!

ORESTES.

This is her husband. He has made her happy.

IPHIGENIA.

This man?— But who—

ORESTES.

A Phocian. Strophius' son.

IPHIGENIA.
Then he is Atreus' grandson! — Our own house!

ORESTES.
Thy cousin; my one friend.

IPHIGENIA.
    As yet unborn
That day I came away to die!

ORESTES.
    The son
Of Strophius in old age.

IPHIGENIA.
    I welcome thee,
My sister's husband.

ORESTES.
    Closer to me than brother.

IPHIGENIA.
But O our mother? — for thou hast not told me —

ORESTES.
Let us not speak of her! — she killed my father.

IPHIGENIA.
Thou hast not told me why.

ORESTES.
Then do not ask me.

IPHIGENIA.
May I not ask if thou art King of Argos?

ORESTES.
Not King but exile.   Menelaus is King.

IPHIGENIA.
What? — in thy time of grief he banished thee?

ORESTES.
Not he but Furies — the avenging Fiends!

IPHIGENIA.
Thy madness on the beach — it was the Fiends?

ORESTES.
Yes, yes!   One seeing me might think me mad.

IPHIGENIA.
And they pursue thee for thy mother's death?

ORESTES.
To catch me and to curb me with her blood!

IPHIGENIA.
Thy coming here?

ORESTES.
>An oracle of Phœbus.

IPHIGENIA.
>Which I may know about?

ORESTES.
>O let me tell
>My bitter narrative from end to end . . .
>>After this poor hand had unspeakably
>Punished my mother's most unspeakable guilt,
>Down on my head they came attacking me,
>The Fiends from Hell. Then Phœbus ordered me
>To Athens, that I might protest their judgment
>At the Tribunal Zeus had sanctified
>To the trial of Ares for some ancient sin.
>>When I arrived there, none of all my friends
>Received me. They avoided me at first
>As one unclean. Later they pitied me
>And gave me food in the same room with them,
>But at a separate table. And they served me
>An equal measure with themselves and filled
>My cup when theirs were filled, but turned
>Away and would not look at me nor speak
>With me — because I was a murderer. . . .
>And I showed no resentment but in silence,
>As though I did not care, I thought of her
>Whom I had killed and drank my bitter cup.
>>They say that the Athenians memorize

My sorrow with a feast, the Pitcher Feast,
In which each man drinks his own cup in si-
    lence. . . .

When I had come to judgment on that hill,
I on one side and on the other side
The eldest of the Avengers charging me
With murder, Phœbus rose to my defence
And by His eloquence redeemed my life.
For Pallas, in the chair, finding the votes
Cast evenly, for and against me, added
Her own vote for me and acquitted me.

Some of the Furies acquiesced and chose
To infest a Temple close to the Tribunal.
Others defied the verdict as unjust
And turned on me again, tormenting me,
Till I fled back to Phœbus for His aid,
Fell down before the Shrine, faint with despair,
And swore to take my life — unless the God
Who had confounded me would rescue me.

And then out pealed His voice, His golden voice
Above the tripod, telling me to go
Among the Taurians, to take away
Their Artemis of stone carven in Heaven
And to establish it and worship it
In Athens.

Help me now to do this thing!
O help me, sister, to obey the God
And carry out His mission! Help me, sister! —
If only I may take within my hands

The image of the Goddess, I am rid
Of madness! And I urge thee with a gift
Of rugged rowers rowing thee back to Argos!
O sister, sister, for our father's house
I beg thy aid, to save that house and me!
Unless we take the Image with thy help,
This very day shall see our house destroyed.

THE FOURTH MAIDEN.
Some God is visiting ancestral sin
    Upon new generations.

IPHIGENIA.
How long, before thy coming, had I dreamed
Of thee and of my country! How I wish
With thee the restoration of our house —
Even his house who would have slain me! Brother,
My heart has melted in our misery.
I have no anger left, but only thought
Of thee escaping and our house revived.
    What can I do? — how hide from Artemis? —
And how put off the King when he perceives
But empty air upon the pedestal?
I am afraid — no, not of death itself
But of the interim, the dying hope. . . .
If we might take the Image and be quick
And flee together on thy leaping ship! —
But we should fail. Yet if I stay to hide
Thy flight, when the discovery is made

— The ravished Image! — Ah but death is good
If by my dying thou returnest home   .   .   .
If a man die — a house, a name, is lost.
But if a woman die — what does it matter?

ORESTES.

It mattered when my mother died. If now
Thy death were added, I should have to take
Two deaths upon my head. Instead of that,
Let come what may, I mean to share thy fate —
Alive in Greece, or here beside thee dead.
    But it is evident the Gods are with us.
If Artemis opposed, should I have been
Expressly sent by Her own Brother here
To bring Her Image back? She wishes it —
For in the very Temple of the Image
As a good omen I have seen thy face!
O what does all this mean but our return?

IPHIGENIA.
How can we steal the Image and not die?

ORESTES.
Can we not kill the King?

IPHIGENIA.
    And dare the Gods
Again? — for he was kind to me.

ORESTES.
And yet
It might be dared — if it would save our lives!

IPHIGENIA.
I like thy boldness. But it cannot be.

ORESTES.
Shall I stay hidden in the shrine till dark?

IPHIGENIA.
And then at night escape?

ORESTES.
Are we not thieves?
The day for honest men, the night for thieves!

IPHIGENIA.
We could not pass the guards.

ORESTES.
What can we do then?

IPHIGENIA.
Perhaps we —

ORESTES.
What?

IPHIGENIA.
May use our own misfortune!

ORESTES.
Women have ways of changing ill to good.

IPHIGENIA.
I shall announce thee as a matricide! . . .

ORESTES.
If there is good in that, make use of it!

IPHIGENIA.
As one unworthy to be sacrificed!

ORESTES.
Thou meanest? — ah but I can guess!

IPHIGENIA.
Unclean,
Unpurified and unacceptable!

ORESTES.
But how does that attain our purpose?

IPHIGENIA.
Pure
Sea-water must be used to cleanse thy sin!

ORESTES.

But that would mean the Image left behind
And all our labor unfulfilled.

IPHIGENIA.

She too,
Having been touched by thy approach, must be
Washed clean, the Image too!

ORESTES.

And might it be —
There, by the inlet —?

IPHIGENIA.

Where thy ship is moored.

ORESTES.

And who will bring the Image? — none but thee?

IPHIGENIA.

For none may ever carry it but me.

ORESTES.

And Pylades? — is he a murderer too?

IPHIGENIA.

He aided thee. He also must be cleansed.

ORESTES.

A story for the guards — but for the King?

IPHIGENIA.

In any case I could not keep it from him.
So he shall hear it and shall be persuaded.

ORESTES.

The oarsmen shall be ready for their orders,
But here ashore thine is the sole command.
    Yet let me ask one question. Will these women
Be true to thee and not betray thee? Pray
For their assistance. Urge them and convince them.
Thou, as a woman, knowest woman well.
Then use the power of thy need of pity . . .
And, after that, let Heaven's high will be done!

IPHIGENIA.

O friends who have been near and dear to me,
I trust you! On you depends my destiny,
Whether I keep or lose my home, my kin.
Woman to women, I appeal to you.
For, knowing our own weakness, we are bound
To feel a woman's need and to defend
Our sex and to be loyal. Will you not
Be silent now for my sake? This is all,
Yes, all I ask of you,— only your silence.
By honoring us, do yourselves honor too!
    See how a single chance is left us three! . . .
Discovery means death. Escape means home!
    If I escape, shall I not work for you
Till I deliver you?— till thou and thou

Shall join me in my joy at home in Hellas —
And thou and thou! I pray thee by thy hand;
Thee by thy cheek; thy knees; thee by thy home;
Thy father and thy mother; thee, thyself
A mother with a child away from thee,
I pray thee by that child: — be merciful!
   O which of you consent? — and which refuse,
When to refuse us means betraying us?

THE FIRST MAIDEN.
   O count upon us, Lady, on our love —
      And go thy way content!
   By Zeus we swear unbroken loyalty.

IPHIGENIA.
   I bless you for those words. I wish you joy.

   (To Orestes and Pylades)

   Now do thy part — and thine. Enter the
      Temple.
   The King will soon be here to make inquiry
   Whether the strangers have been sacrificed.

   (Orestes and Pylades go into the Temple)

   Grim Goddess, having saved me once before,
   Now save me with my brother and his friend,
   Lest Phœbus be disproved because of Thee

And men forsake His oracle!   O come
In gracious might away from this bleak place,
Away from gloom — to Athens and to glory!

(She follows into the Temple)

THE SECOND MAIDEN.
 O sad-voiced ocean-bird, heard in the foam
  Low by the rocky ledge
 Singing a note unhappy hearts can hear,
 The song of separation from thy mate,
  The moan of separation,
 I have no wings to seek like thee, but I
  Can sing a song like thee,
 A song of separation from my mates.

 At home in Hellas now are gathering
  My kinsmen.   Artemis
 Blesses the new-born from Her Cynthian hill
 And soothes the mothers with the cooling palm
  And bay and olive-tree,
 Where once Latona loved the winding streams
  And watched the rounded pools
 White with the song-like motion of the swans.

 Alas! the falling tears, the towers fallen,
  The taking of our towns!
 Alas! the clash of bright and angry spears
 That captured me aboard an alien ship! —

Whence I was sold away
To be an exile here, a handmaiden
   With Agamemnon's daughter,
Doomed to the bloody rites of Artemis.

THE FOURTH MAIDEN.
And at these altars where the sacrifice
   Is not of sheep but men,
I envy those unhappy from their birth;
For to be bred and seasoned in misfortune
   Is to be iron to it. . . .
O there is something in the pang of change
   More than the heart can bear —
Unhappily remembering happiness.

THE FIRST MAIDEN.
Lady, a ship is here to take thee home,
   And in the rowers' ears
Pan shall be sounding all his pointed notes,
Great mountains echoing to his little reed,
   And Phœbus on his lyre
Shall strike profound the seven strings and sing
   To thee of Attica,
Shall sing to thee of home and lead thee there.

Oar after oar shall dip and carry thee,
   Lady, away from me,
Oar after oar shall push the empty sea
Wider, wider, leaving me lonely here,

Leaving me here without thee.
And forward over the unceasing bow
   Thy sail shall faster run,
Ever refilling with the unspent wind.

THE SECOND MAIDEN.
  O to go swiftly like the wingèd sun
    Upon his dazzling track
  And not to let my golden light be folded
  Until I touched my house, my roof, my room!
    Then I should go again
  To noble marriages and take my place
    In the bright company,
  Give them my hands and circle round and dance.

And I should strive to be the loveliest
    In all my looks and ways,
In my unrivalled brightness of attire
And in the motion of my hands and feet;
    And my embroidered veil
I should hold closely round me as I danced
    And I should hide my cheek
In the soft shadow of my clustering curls.

(Enter King Thoas with Soldiers)

THOAS.
  Where is the keeper of the Temple-gates,
  The maid of Hellas? Is her labor done? —

Are the victims' bodies burning in the shrine?

A MAIDEN.
See where she comes, to answer thee herself.

(Iphigenia comes out of the Temple, carrying the Image)

THOAS.
What does this mean, daughter of Agamemnon?
Why hast thou brought the Image from its place?

IPHIGENIA.
O King, stand back! — stand back beyond the threshold!

THOAS.
Is it some new observance in the Temple?

IPHIGENIA.
Stay back, I tell thee, from Her holy presence!

THOAS.
I will stay back, but tell me, tell me why
Thou bearest Her like this.

IPHIGENIA.
The sacrifice
Thou gavest to the Goddess was unclean.

THOAS.
How dost thou know? — what makes thee think —

IPHIGENIA.
    She turned
Away from them,— away when they approached.

THOAS.
Might it not be some tremor of the ground
That moved Her.

IPHIGENIA.
    No.   By Her own will She moved —
And even for a moment shut Her eyes.

THOAS.
Because of blood upon the strangers' hands?

IPHIGENIA.
It was Her divination of their guilt.

THOAS.
Whose blood?   A Taurian's blood? — killed on the
    beach?

IPHIGENIA.
The guilt was with them when they came; the stain
Of killing their own kin!

THOAS.

Their kin? What kin?

IPHIGENIA.

A mother! — whom they murdered in cold blood!

THOAS.

O great Apollo, what barbarian
Would do the thing these Greeks have done?

IPHIGENIA.

But Greeks
Disowned and homeless, hunted out of Hellas.

THOAS.

Even then why bring the Image here?

IPHIGENIA.

Defiled,
She must be purified, be touched again
By Her own firmament.

THOAS.

How dost thou know
So well the nature of their infamy?

IPHIGENIA.

Seeing Her turn away, I asked them why.

THOAS.

Thou art a Greek, quick-witted, a true Greek!

IPHIGENIA.

They too are Greeks. They thought they could
    appease me
With pleasant news.

THOAS.

    Of Argos?

IPHIGENIA.

    Of my brother,
News of Orestes.

THOAS.

    To inveigle thee!

IPHIGENIA.

And of my father — that he lives and prospers.

THOAS.

Thou hadst no doubt, however, of thy duty?

IPHIGENIA.

Has not all Hellas well deserved my hate?

THOAS.

What must we do with them?

IPHIGENIA.
    Observe the law.

THOAS.
    Thou meanest with the water and the knife?

IPHIGENIA.
    First fully cleanse them of their sin.

THOAS.
    With water
    From a bubbling spring or from the salty sea?

IPHIGENIA.
    The sea is the absolvent of all evil.

THOAS.
    The sea would better please the Goddess then?

IPHIGENIA.
    And me.

THOAS.
    The breakers almost reach these walls.

IPHIGENIA.
    But certain of the rites are secret rites.

THOAS.
    Then choose thy place and fear no trespasser.

IPHIGENIA.
  And I must purify the Image too.

THOAS.
  Have they contaminated even Her?

IPHIGENIA.
  So that I had to bring Her from Her place.

THOAS.
  Thanks for thy reverential care.

IPHIGENIA.
    O King,
  Command the help I need.

THOAS.
    Ask — it is given.

IPHIGENIA.
  Then let the strangers be well bound.

THOAS.
    Why that?
  Where could they think to flee?

IPHIGENIA.
  Beware of Greeks!

THOAS.

   (To his Servants)

  Go, bind them.

IPHIGENIA.
  Have them brought to me.

THOAS.
  And bring them.

IPHIGENIA.
  But hang a heavy veil over their heads.

THOAS.
  For they must not be witnessed by the sun.

IPHIGENIA.
  Send soldiers with me.

THOAS.
  Choose thy guard from these.

IPHIGENIA.
  And let a herald warn all citizens.

THOAS.
  Of what?

IPHIGENIA.
  To stay indoors till this is done.

THOAS.
Lest they as well might suffer the contagion?

IPHIGENIA.
From matricide.

THOAS.
Go tell the herald this.

IPHIGENIA.
And anyone I care for —

THOAS.
Meaning — me?

IPHIGENIA.
Him above all I caution against harm,
Not to come near.

THOAS.
Thou carest what we do.

IPHIGENIA.
Thou seest.

THOAS.
And what thou dost means much to us.

IPHIGENIA.
Wait here, O King — thy share is in the Temple.

THOAS.
   To —

IPHIGENIA.
   Purify it with the smoke of torches.

THOAS.
   It shall be fragrant, priestess, to receive thee.

IPHIGENIA.
   When they come by —

THOAS.
   What must I do?

IPHIGENIA.
   Hold up
   Thy robe and look away.

THOAS.
   From the contagion.

IPHIGENIA.
   And if I seem delayed —

THOAS.
   How shall I tell?

IPHIGENIA.
   Be not surprised, but patient.

THOAS.

Take thy time
And serve the Goddess to the uttermost.

IPHIGENIA.

If it but end as I desire! —

THOAS.

And I!

IPHIGENIA.

Ah, here they come! — the strangers and the robes,
And lambs whose blood shall offset other blood,
And burning torches and all instruments
Purification needs for them and Her.

Away, O citizens, be not polluted!
You keepers of the gates, keep clean your hands!
Men who would marry, women who would bear,
Be not polluted! — look away — away!

O Virgin Goddess, if these murderers
Be cleansed as I would have them cleansed and Thou
Be brought as well where I would have Thee
        brought,
Thy Temple shall be clean and we be blest!
I say no more — but Thou and those who know
May render the conclusion of my prayer.

(The procession passes out. Thoas enters the Temple)

THE THIRD MAIDEN.
Latona bore one day a golden Child,
    O Artemis, Thy Brother,
Phœbus, the darling of the vales of Delos —

THE FIRST MAIDEN.
Whose little fingers hovered on the harp
    And pulled at archery.

THE THIRD MAIDEN.
Leaving His birthplace, to Parnassus' top
    The Mother brought Her Boy —

THE SECOND MAIDEN.
Where Dionysus flings the waterfall.

THE THIRD MAIDEN.
There hidden coiling in the leafy laurels
    A serpent, with bright scales
And blood-red eyes, a creature born of Earth,
Guarded the cave that held Earth's oracle.
    Phœbus, beholding it, leaped up
Out of His Mother's arms, a little Child,
    And struck the serpent dead —

THE SECOND MAIDEN.
And on that day began His prophecies.

THE FOURTH MAIDEN.
  Phœbus Apollo, Thou hast won the throne,
    The tripod of the truth!
  And in the very centre of the earth
  Thou hearest wisdom; and Thy voice conveys,
    Accompanied by all
  The run and ripple of Castalian springs,
    The inmost oracles
  That ever Heaven whispered to the Earth.

THE THIRD MAIDEN.
  But Earth had wished the oracles to go
    To Themis, Her own daughter,
  And in Her anger bred a band of dreams
  That in the night should be oracular
    To men, foretelling truth.
  And this impaired the dignity of Phœbus
    And of His oracles —

THE SECOND MAIDEN.
  And the baby God went hurrying to Zeus,
  Coaxed with His little hands and begged of Zeus
    To send the dreams away .   .   .

THE FIRST MAIDEN.
  And He was very pleased to have His son
  Come straight to Him with troubles. And His
      head
    Decided with a nod

That men should turn from the prophetic dark
  And every haunting shape —

THE FOURTH MAIDEN.
  And listen only to the lips of Light.

A MESSENGER.

  (Entering breathless)

  O all you ministers and temple-guards,
  Where is King Thoas gone? Open the gates
  And call King Thoas out! O call the King!

THE FIRST MAIDEN.
  If we may ask unbidden — is something wrong?

THE MESSENGER.
  The two young men have broken free and fled,
  With Agamemnon's daughter aiding them —
  And on their ship have taken Artemis!

THE FIRST MAIDEN.
  A likely story! — Wouldst thou find the King,
  He left the Temple but a moment since.

THE MESSENGER.
  Where was he bound?

THE FIRST MAIDEN.
   I do not know which way.

THE SECOND MAIDEN.
   Go look for him, go find him with thy story!

THE MESSENGER.
   O treacherous women! You would put me off,
   You are in the plot yourselves!

THE THIRD MAIDEN.
   Art thou gone mad?
   What are these men to us? Quick! To the
       Palace!

THE MESSENGER.
   Not till I know to my own satisfaction,
   Not till I rouse the keepers of the Shrine
   To answer me! Ho! You inside! Unbar
   The door! The King, if he is there, tell him
   A messenger has come with evil news!

   (He beats at the door)

THOAS.

   (Appearing at the Temple-Door)

Who makes this outcry, desecrates the door
And shakes this holy place?

THE MESSENGER.
     Their fault! — their fault!
They told me thou wert absent from the Temple,
They put me off from finding thee.

THOAS.
     But why?
Why should they wish —

THE MESSENGER.
     Let that come afterward.
O listen first to what I have to tell! —
Iphigenia who was priestess here
Has joined the strangers, fled with them and taken
Artemis' Image! — the cleansing was a lie!

THOAS.
     Unthinkable! — What evil influence —

THE MESSENGER.
     The chance to save Orestes — yes, Orestes!

THOAS.
     Orestes? — which Orestes? Not her brother?

THE MESSENGER.
     Yes, whom the Goddess wanted for Her altar.

THOAS.
     It is impossible, I cannot grasp it!

THE MESSENGER.

    But do not stop to grasp it! — listen first,
    Consider what to do! — and then command
    What means may intercept and capture them!

THOAS.

    There is no danger in these Taurian Seas
    Of their escaping. For the way is shut —
    Stationed and cordoned with a ring of ships!

THE MESSENGER.

    No sooner had we reached the bend of shore
    Which hid their ship, than Agamemnon's daughter
    Made signs to us to drop the rope that bound
    The men, to leave them and fall back. It seemed
    That she was ready to perform the rites,
    To light the mystic flame and bless the sea.
    She took the rope herself and followed them
    Still further. And we felt presentiment
    Of something wrong. But what were we to do?
    We heard her voice chant a high mystery
    Of phrases in an unknown tongue, seeming
    To us the ceremonial incantation,
    The ritual of purifying sin.
    And then we waited a long time. At last
    The fear occurred to us that they had burst
    Their bonds, had killed her and escaped. But still
    We waited, fearing with an equal fear
    To see what was forbidden us to see . . .

Until with one accord agreeing to it
We disobeyed and went to find them.
  There
We saw the ship from Hellas near the shore,
And fitted in the tholes were fifty oars
Like feathers in a wing, and just astern
The two youths boarding her. Some held the prow
With poles thrust in the water, others brought
The anchor up. The rest had made of rope
A ladder hanging from the rail. By this
We knew their scheme. And we laid hold at once
Of the Greek maid and seized the trailing ladder
And pulled their rudder-oar away from them
To cripple them and cried: "What treachery
Is this? — to steal our priestess and our God?
Who art thou and whose son to raid our land
And bear our priestess off?" And he replied:
"I am Orestes, son of Agamemnon,
I am her brother. Now you know the truth.
And she is bound for Greece, out of which land
I lost her long ago — bound home!"
  We clung
To her and meant to drag her from her friends
To thee; which is the way I came by these,
This bruise — and this. They struck my face both
    sides.
They had no weapons, we had none. We used
Our fists and they their fists, even their feet
With kicks well-aimed at us from where they stood

Above us — at our heads and sides. We fought
Till we were breathless. Then, with bruises
And cuts and blood-filled eyes, we climbed the cliff
And, from our vantage, pelted them with stones —
Till the Greek archers had arranged their bows
And kept us a distance with their arrows.

Then when a giant wave bore them inshore,
Orestes quickly lifted up his sister
Out of the rush of it. Holding her high
On his left shoulder, plunging stride by stride,
He caught the ladder, swung aboard the ship
And held her safe on deck. And she, she held —
She had it still — the Image out of Heaven,
The Image of the Daughter of high Zeus!

Then a glad call exulted through the ship:
" O mariners of Hellas, grip your oars
And clip the sea to foam! O let your arms
Be strong, for we have won, have won, have won
What we set out to win! We have defied
The jagged Clashing Rocks — and we have won! "

A shout of joy responded and the ship
Quivered with dipping oars and shot ahead.
But this was only while the shelter lasted;
For at the harbor-mouth a high wave met her
And threw her off her course. She turned about,
Caught by the stormy wind, until her stern
Was foremost and her prow toward shore. They
    tugged
The oars, rallied and strained — but every time

They brought her round, the deep wave dragged her
    back
Again. And Agamemnon's daughter stood
And prayed: "O save me, Artemis, from this
Unhappy place — to Hellas! — and forgive
My theft! As Thou, O Goddess, lovest well
Phœbus, Thy brother, shall I not love mine?"
    The sailors' praises echoing her prayer,
They bent their bodies and their great bare arms
And shoulders, swaying like the sea,
To the boatswain's cry. But closer to the cliff,
Closer and closer still they drew. And some
Sprang out into the sea. And some began
Attempts to fasten hold on the sharp shore
With ropes. And then our men despatched me
    here,
O King, to tell thee of this thing. . . . So come
With chains and cords — for while the sea is high,
There is no earthly chance of their escape!

Poseidon, God of the Sea, remembering Troy,
The city that He loved, confounds today
The wretched children of her enemies
And will deliver up to thee and thine
The son and daughter of the King of Argos —
That daughter who, forgetful now of Aulis,
Betrays the Goddess who was kind to her.

    (*The Messenger goes out*)

THE FIRST MAIDEN.

O Lady, Lady! — O alas for thee!
  In Taurian hands again,
Thou and thy brother surely now shall die!

THOAS.

Come, citizens, and be uncivilized!
Leap on your horses! Whip them to the beach!
Wait with me there until a wave shall break
That ship from Hellas. Then — be after them!
And hunt them down, each damnèd dog of
    them!
Do this for Artemis. And some of you
Go launch my galleys, lest one man of them
Should die untortured! Run them down by sea
And land! Go hurl them from the cliffs!
O catch them, kill them, crucify them, end them!

And as for you, you miserable women,
Count on the punishment you have deserved
By treachery! I have not time for you —
With this to do. But O when this is done!

(*In the confusion appears, with instant dominion,
    Pallas Athena*)

ATHENA.

Be calm, King Thoas! What is this pursuit?
Hold back and listen to Athena's word.

Hold back the soldiers, hold them every one.
Apollo sent Orestes to this land
To free him from the Fiends of punishment
And told him, through the oracle, to bring
Iphigenia home again to Argos
And likewise to my land the holy Image. . . .
That is my word. And let me follow it
With news that this Orestes thou wouldst hunt
Is gliding on a comfortable sea
Made easy by Poseidon for my sake.

Orestes! — thou canst hear a God far-off —
Obey me! Take thy sister and the Image
Safely to Hellas. Go to God-built Athens
And, passing through, go forward to the end
Of Attica. Find there a holy place
Close to Carystus' hill, a place called Halae.
There build a Temple. There set up the Image.
Name it for Tauris, to immortalize
Thy penitence and thy deliverance,
Thy labors and thy love. Let men acclaim
The Taurian Artemis, brought there by thee.
    And let this be the law: When they observe
Her festival . . . in token of thy fate
The priest must hold against a human throat
The sharp blade of his knife and touch the edge
With blood, then cease — meaning that life, not
    death,
Is the true element of sacrifice.

Iphigenia! — there are steps for thee
Hewn to the rocky Shrine of Artemis
At Brauron.   There the keys be in thy keeping.
There shalt thou die, be buried and receive
Upon thy grave most honorable gifts,
The purely-woven raiment of dead mothers
Who honorably died in giving birth.

O Thoas, I command thee, send to Hellas
These women.   They were true.—
    I saved thee once,
Orestes, when on Ares' hill I judged thee
And voted for thee when the votes were equal.
Now let it be the law that he who earns
An equally-divided verdict wins
His case.   Therefore go safely from this land,
O son of Agamemnon.   And thou, Thoas,
Be thou content to put thy wrath away.

THOAS.

He who is discontented when the Gods
Have given judgment — is a fool.   For my part,
Goddess, I bear no grudge against Orestes
Nor against her who took away the Image.
I make no opposition to a God,
For where would be the use?   So let them go
In peace and set the Image in Thy land.
These women too may go — they shall be sent
To Hellas to be happy.   At Thy word,

I bid my ships turn back from the pursuit . . .
Behold my spirit and my spear bowed down.

ATHENA.
  Well-spoken! For thy spirit learns a law
  Greater than thou and greater than the Gods.

  O winds of heaven, blow Orestes home —
  And I will guide him on his way to Athens,
  Guarding Thy Image, Artemis, my Sister.

THE FIRST MAIDEN.
  Fare well in your good-fortune! May it bring
    Joy to you always.

THE FOURTH MAIDEN.
  Pallas Athena, blessed is Thy name
    In Heaven as on the earth.
  Let us be mindful that Thy words are wise
  And welcome and unlooked-for and complete
    And let us do Thy will,
  O Conqueror of hatred and of fear! . . .
    The more in Thee we lose
  Our lives, the more we find our life in Thee.

THE END